AF817070

Marx in London

An Illustrated Guide

My part of this book is for Pilvi, who came into my life, so unexpectedly, in Copenhagen with a dream of Marx; and who, I hope, will not leave it again.

John Callow

Marx in London

An Illustrated Guide

Asa Briggs
John Callow

AAKAR

MARX IN LONDON: An Illustrated Guide
Asa Briggs and John Callow

© Lawrence and Wishart 2008
© Aakar Books for South Asia 2015

First Published in India 2015

ISBN 978-93-5002-359-4

Published in agreement with Lawrence and Wishart Limited, London for publication and sale only in the Indian Subcontinent (India, Pakistan, Bangladesh, Nepal, Maldives, Bhutan and Sri Lanka)

All rights reserved. No part of this book may be reproduced or transmitted, in any form or by any means, without the prior permission of the publisher.

Published by
AAKAR BOOKS
28 E Pocket IV, Mayur Vihar Phase I, Delhi 110 091
Phone : 011 2279 5505 Telefax : 011 2279 5641
aakarbooks@gmail.com; www.aakarbooks.com

Printed at
Sapra Brothers, Delhi 110 092

Contents

Preface and acknowledgements

Thousands of visitors to twenty-first century London, coming from all parts of the world, are interested in seeing the places in the city with which Marx was particularly associated in his life time; not surprisingly, therefore, this book is not the first of its kind. As early as 1948, a booklet, *London Landmarks*, was published to commemorate the centenary of the *Communist Manifesto* (republished in 1963). Since it was likely to soon go out of print, and to celebrate the centenary of Marx's death, in 1982 I wrote *Marx in London: An Illustrated Guide*, in conjunction with a series of television programmes, with John Dekker, John Mair and Ian Taylor as producers. It was translated into several languages.

This new Guide, written collaboratively with John Callow, Librarian of the Marx Memorial Library, is intended not only for visitors to London from overseas but for British visitors to London who are still looking for the missing Marx, and, equally important, for readers of Marx wherever they live, many of whom may not be able to travel to London but who are concerned to find out more about his life in the city, a more complex life than his writings may suggest.

The guide sets out useful information, both biographical and typographical, and is fully illustrated with photographs, maps and other illustrations, many of them new; some of them show how the places which Marx knew best have changed since his death in 1883. It deals also with some of Marx's communist successors, who had their own connections with London. These include Vladimir Ilych Lenin, who in 1901-1902 shared an editorial office at 37/38 Clerkenwell Green, now Marx House (the home of the Marx Memorial Library), from which he published a series of issues of *Iskra*, the Russian Social Democratic newspaper.

This new Guide has been published through Marx House just as the 1982 Guide was published through the BBC. Without the enterprising initiative of my co-author, John Callow, who appreciated the potential in a new volume on Marx in London and has followed his own

Marx trail through the London of the early twenty-first century, it would never have appeared. We both owe a great debt to Sally Davison of Lawrence and Wishart, deeply committed to the venture, and to my personal assistant in all my ventures, Pat Spencer, who has acted as an intermediary.

Asa Briggs, October 2007

Photo acknowledgements

Pictures on pages 68 (bottom), 100 (bottom): ©John Callow

Pictures on pages 9, 10, 12, 19, 20, 22, 23, 24, 25, 26, 27, 29, 35 (bottom), 38 (both), 41 (top), 43, 46, 53 (both), 55, 61, 63, 64 (all), 67, 68 (top), 70, 71, 73, 74, 76, 83 (top), 84, 85, 86, 89, 90 (both), 93, 101: courtesy Marx Memorial Library

Pictures on pages 30, 31 (both), 35 (top), 41 (bottom), 42 (both), 47, 48 (both), 51, 58, 62, 78, 79, 83 (bottom), 97, 98, 99, 100 (top), 103: © Andrew Wiard

Special thanks to Andrew Wiard, who took most of the new pictures for this book, and who has devoted his talents over many years to the chronicling of the British labour movement.

1. The missing Marx

The role of Karl Marx (1818-1883) cannot be ignored in any account of the history of the modern world. Nor can the message that he proclaimed, first set out in the most famous manifesto in history, *The Communist Manifesto*. This was originally drawn up in German a few weeks before the 1848 Revolution in France, but was eventually printed in London, where Marx himself lived as a political exile from 1849. After this first call to arms, Marx continued for the rest of his life to write on political economy and a wide range of social and political ideas, devoting his life to the task of not only explaining the world but also changing it.

Though born in Trier in Germany's Rhineland, Marx spent most of his adult life in London. At that time it was Europe's biggest city, a modern 'Babylon', with large numbers of exiles – a city constantly in physical change, then as now. Marx lived in various places in the capital, from 1849 until his death on 14 March 1883, and then he was buried in Highgate Cemetery in the north of the city. Every year since 1933 there has been a commemorative oration at the graveside on 14 March, organised by the Marx Memorial Library, and taking place in rain or sunshine. (The tomb was moved to a better position in the cemetery in 1954, with a new sculpted memorial added in 1956.)

Many world events have been registered in these graveside addresses, including two world wars when Britain and Germany were on opposite sides. The twentieth century also saw the rise and fall of communist states, influenced by the Leninist approach to Marxism, and many of their leaders visited the graveside. For some the collapse of communism has proved Marx wrong. Others argue that his analysis of the workings of capitalism has never been superseded: the accuracy of his predictions of the spread of capitalism and commodity production across the globe is all too evident at the beginning of the twenty-first century. Whatever position one takes, it is impossible to deny that Marx and what he stands for remain relevant for any understanding of the twentieth or the twenty-first century. Marx's ideas have had influence not just through the governments for whom (rightly or wrongly) he was a source of inspiration, but through the millions of people who struggle against injustice across the world.

The Missing Marx?

A stunning mural, recalling Soho's past, was unveiled in Broadwick Street – off fashionable Carnaby Street – by the Freeform Arts Trust in 1991. Marx was one of the mechanised figures activated by the clock at its centre. However, by the summer of 2006, the mechanism had broken and the clock had stopped. Marx was taken down from the wall, and a void created.

Ironically, when Marx died only a small proportion of working people in Britain had ever heard of his name, and fewer still had been able to read his voluminous writings, three quarters of which were not published until after his death. Alan Booth, one of the speakers at the graveside commemoration in 1983, talked about the missing Marx: despite his massive influence, Marx's life in London is only sparsely commemorated.

The names of Marx and Lenin have been closely associated since the Bolshevik Revolution in Russia in 1917, and the 'ism' of Marxism-Leninism has been used almost as much as the 'ism' of Marxism. Yet Marx and Lenin came from quite different countries with quite different traditions, and in Marx's lifetime his name was most frequently associated with that of his fellow German revolutionary Friedrich Engels (1820-1895).

Born in a small industrial town in the Rhineland where his father ran a cotton yarn factory, Engels visited Manchester – already a smoky and noisy industrial city – in 1842, staying there and working in a branch of his father's firm until August 1844. Manchester at that time was a shock city, which everyone who wished to understand what was happening to society in the age of steam felt compelled to visit. Engels's own book *The Condition of the Working Class in England*, published in Leipzig in 1845, was based on his reflections on life in Manchester. In focusing on the textile industry, the source of Manchester's wealth, and on the class struggle between employers and workers, it was directly related to the economic and political analysis in Marx's own work. The life-time cooperation of Marx and Engels began in 1844: 'When I visited Marx in Paris in the summer of 1844', Engels wrote later, 'we found ourselves in complete agreement on questions of theory and our collaboration began at that time'. In almost forty years of partnership, with Engels giving crucial financial support to Marx, they were as close in their thinking and feeling as any two people could be, and their correspondence is an invaluable historical source.

Frederick Engels, in the mid-1840s

This is the earliest photograph of Engels, though the place in which it was taken, and the name of the photographer are unknown. Having completed his military service in Berlin, so that he might attend lectures at the university there, Engels worked as an office clerk at his father's cotton factory in Manchester, in 1842–44. It was there that he observed, first hand, the impact of the Industrial Revolution and began to draft his seminal account of The Condition of the Working Class in England, *which was published in Leipzig in 1845, shortly before the author's twenty-fifth birthday.*

Nineteenth-century London is usually referred to in our own century as Victorian London, but mid-Victorian London has also been described – rightly – as the London of Charles Dickens (1812-1870), and many of today's visitors, including those particularly interested in Marx, often start with a picture of Dickens's London in mind. Indeed no other single writer has done more to perpetuate in his writings the sense of Victorian London. Yet it is important to realise that London changed greatly, both during his own lifetime and, even more, between 1870 and 1901. To discover what remains of Dickens's London requires as much exploration, preferably on foot, as does the discovery of the London of Marx. There is much to see, however, especially if you know where to look. Every explorer will draw their own map, and no two maps are quite alike, but it is hoped that this guide will prove useful to all.

There were many foreign political exiles in Britain at that time, particularly following the failure of the European revolutions of 1848, but London was the place in England where most of them congregated. Nevertheless it is important to remember that London provoked ambivalent reactions on the part of the exiles who settled here in the nineteenth century. Thus, Alexander Herzen, the Russian revolutionary, who arrived in London in 1852, complained three years later that London life was 'about as boring as that of worms in a cheese'. Yet two years after that he told a Swiss friend, 'beyond all manner of doubt, England, with all the follies of Feudalism and Toryism which are peculiar to it, is the only country to live in'.

Marx himself could often feel a satisfying isolation in the midst of English society and politics. 'I am greatly pleased by the public, authentic isolation in which we too, you and I now find ourselves', he wrote to Engels in 1851, the year of London's Great Exhibition, when thousands of foreigners visited London. The isolation, he added was 'wholly in accord with our attitude and principles'.

Yet Marx could also be a sociable being, and he shared many of the common experiences of London Victorian life. Furthermore, his daughter, Eleanor (1855-1898) was born in Britain and was a British citizen; and Marx himself applied for naturalisation, though he was refused it, in 1874. William Liebknecht (1826-1900), who knew the Marx family well, has given a graphic account of their life in London in his book *Karl Marx: Biographical Memoirs* (1896). Having first lived in London as a political exile during the 1850s, Liebknecht returned from Germany in 1878, comparing himself with the archaeologist Schliemann when he set out to excavate Troy. He immediately discerned that the revolution which had taken place since he had previously been in London was topographical, not ideological, and he was prepared to generalise from it: 'What revolutionary changes in the modern great cities', he observed. 'It is a continual uprooting – although, as in political revolutions also, not everywhere, not in all parts. And a man starting today from a modern great city on a tour of the world will not be able on his return to find his way through a good many quarters.'

On arriving back in London after an absence of sixteen years, Liebknecht went on, he had rubbed his eyes. 'Was this the city in which I have lived for nearly half a generation and of which I then knew every street, every corner?' he asked.

'Streets gone, sections disappeared – new streets, new buildings, and the general aspect so changed that in a place where I formerly could have made my way blindfolded I had to take refuge in a cab in order to get to my near goal.'

There must have been many visitors to late-Victorian London who shared Liebknecht's reactions. Not everywhere had changed, however, and Liebknecht ended his tour on Hampstead Heath, lunching at the public house, Jack Straw's Castle. 'How many hundred times had we been here? And in the same room where we were sitting today, I had been sitting – long, long ago – dozens of times with Marx, with Mrs Marx, with the children, with Lenchen, the family maid, and others. And the past returned.'

When Marx first came to London to live in 1849, his own past involved very different German associations – Trier, surrounded by vineyards and wooded hills, once a Roman headquarters; the university town of Bonn, briefly to be a twentieth-century capital; Berlin, capital of Prussia, city of police, soldiers and spies, but the city where Marx had first encountered the philosophy of Hegel. And there were non-German elements in his experience too. He had lived for a year and a half in Paris, a city of wealth (and corruption) as brilliantly described by his favourite novelist, Balzac, as London was by Dickens – and associated with revolution, as London was not. He had also lived in Belgium, where, as in Britain, there was substantial early industrialisation.

Marx was now separated physically from that experience, but he never became so preoccupied with London – or England – that the English connection changed his attitudes and his feelings. It provided him with data and with ideas – and with basic security to study and to live – but for the

Marx in London, early May 1861

Marx sent a copy of this photo to Engels, in Manchester, on 10 May 1861. Evidently, this rather stern portrait was not to his wife's taste, as Jenny Marx complained to a friend that: 'it is not a good one, and the girls are now determined to have another done'.

application of what he found out he always looked to a far wider scene. He also travelled back to continental Europe on many occasions, including three trips in 1874, 1875 and 1876, for health reasons, to Karlsbad (now in the Czech Republic, and known as Karlovy Vary (see p71)).

Wherever Marx travelled – and whatever his reasons – he always analysed the political and economic processes of the places in which he found himself. Immediately after his arrival in London in 1849 he assured a friend that 'a tremendous industrial, agricultural and commercial crisis was approaching in England', and that, 'even against its will', England might become 'an ally of the revolutionary continent'.

2. The London Marx found

The London Marx came to in 1849 was already a huge city of two-and-a-half million people, a vast built-up area stretching nine miles from Fulham in the west to the riverside town of Poplar in the east, and seven miles from Highgate in the north to Camberwell in the south.

It was still largely a Georgian city, comprising the ancient cities of London (the City) and Westminster, and the districts of Bloomsbury, Mayfair, Marylebone, Holborn, Islington, Shoreditch, Bethnal Green, Bow and Southwark, very different in their social composition and physical appearance. It also had more clearly defined limits than later in the century, although it was already by the 1820s what William Cobbett, the radical writer, called, sarcastically, a 'great' or 'an infernal' Wen.

The radical writer and publisher G.W.M. Reynolds began his highly popular volumes *The Mysteries of London* in 1846 with a lurid prologue in which he referred both to London's 'boundless magnitude' and its 'fearful contrasts'. 'A thousand towers pointed upwards from horizon to horizon'. Yet 'the most unbounded wealth' was 'the neighbour of the most hideous poverty' and 'the most gorgeous pomp' was placed in relief by 'the most deplorable squalor'.

Within the great Wen, the London that mattered most was *north* of the Thames. The nation's financial centre, including the Bank of England and the Stock Exchange, was located in the City proper. North of the Thames, too, were the cultural, business and administrative centres – Whitehall, Parliament, the courts and the palace. However, there were important tracts of common land south of the river, including the commons at Kennington and further away at Clapham; and there was Lambeth Palace, the London home of the Archbishop of Canterbury.

House building had had its ups and downs, with a huge boom during the 1820s in the western districts adjacent to London, a development that reached and engulfed nearby villages like Paddington. One name – since lost – Tyburnia, derived from Tyburn Tree (now Marble Arch), was applied to an area which included Paddington, Bayswater, Notting Hill and North Kensington. Another area, Belgravia, was to spread out in the 1850s to Chelsea, Pimlico and Victoria (although the railway station named after the Queen was not opened until 1860).

There had been significant changes in London's economic and political life before 1849. In particular, its industries had already declined, while those of the Midlands and the north of England had increased in size and volume of output. The old silk industry of Spitalfields, for example, was by now a problem industry, distinguished for its 'demoralised condition'. Yet important industrial activities remained and indeed expanded in London – among them printing, engineering and the manufacture of consumer goods, like matches, clothing, ale and soap. And, if there was less of a sense of 'class' in London than there was in the industrial north, with its factories and furnaces, there were highly-organised London 'trades', groups of workers associated collectively, with the shoemakers largest in numbers and the tailors second. There was also a popular radical tradition with less dependence on – indeed, belief in – organised religion than there was in the north.

Finally, given the rate of change in London, building was a major activity, and it too encouraged workers' association. Even before Queen Victoria came to the throne, there were many massive construction projects in London – streets, docks and, later, railways and tunnels. The great new system of underground sewers, an enormous engineering feat, had not begun to be built, however, when Marx arrived – London was deliberately excluded from the provisions of England's first national Public Health Act in 1848 – nor had work started on the Thames Embankment.

The River Thames, an important stimulus to the imagination of Dickens, had for centuries shaped London's history, linking the city with Europe but dividing England itself. It was a polluted river, not least outside the buildings of Parliament. Even there the stench could be appalling. Yet river transport was maintained, with steamers carrying 125 passengers plying backwards and forwards between London Bridge and Westminster all day from 8 am to 9 pm.

Moving from one part of London to another, except on foot, was not easy – or cheap – for many Londoners when Marx arrived. The first Underground station was not opened until 1863, and the horse bus, while commonplace, was still a relative novelty. The first two omnibuses, hauled by three horses, had been introduced in 1829 by George Shillibeer, a British-born coachbuilder, who had lived in Paris. They plied between Paddington Green along the New Road – now Marylebone and Euston Road – and past the Angel, Islington, to the Bank of England; by 1849 there were 620 of them. It was already possible to travel from Charing Cross to Camden Town for one penny, and there were many threepenny fares. Yet it was not until

1856, with the foundation of the London General Omnibus Company, that small operators, seeking custom on profitable routes, gave way to the large fleet owners offering a general service.

Given the difficulties of transport, merchants and lawyers, as well as clerks, and most warehousemen and artisans, might still walk to work. Even the City of London retained its character as a place to live as well as work, although it was soon to become the 'ghost city' at nightfall when the thousands of office workers went back to the suburbs. The railways were already arriving before Queen Victoria came to the throne, for in 1836 the Deptford line to London Bridge Station was complete. Euston Station was opened in 1837 and Waterloo Station in 1848 (Kings Cross was to follow in 1852).

Railways did more to change the appearance and social life of cities than any other innovation, though their effects were complex and controversial. They led to huge investment – and employment – but also to wild speculation; to new warehouses and stations, but also to large-scale clearing of old houses; ultimately to more democratic modes of travel, but also to the creation of new social and physical divides, 'the two sides of the track'; to the large scale movement of goods, which made many of them cheaper, but to the spread of luxuries also; and, not least, to a new sense of time. Railways were associated both with regularity and punctuality (*Bradshaw*, the book of railway timetables, first appeared in 1839) and, more disturbingly, with a speeding-up of life, and with inevitable accidents on the way. The peak year of construction of new lines was 1846, and of miles of track completed 1848. The financial crash of 1847, which lay in the background of the European revolutions of 1848, was often attributed to railway speculation.

Migration to London from other parts of the country had long preceded the coming of the railway, and in a decade of increased migration, Marx himself was only one of a large number of immigrants from both inside and outside Britain. Indeed, in the ten years between the Census of 1841 and 1851 some 330,000 newcomers arrived in London. There were sharp contrasts of experience and fortune among them. A few were to become rich through trade or connections. Larger numbers, however, were to become artisans or domestic servants, whose 'upstairs-downstairs' contrasts persisted until after the end of the reign of Queen Victoria. Some immigrants moved downwards rather than upwards. No fewer than 120,000 people were evicted from their old homes between 1853 and 1900 as the railways and then the Underground were extended. Nor were the poor ever eliminated, though they might often be moved from one place to another: 'The poor', *The Times* wrote in 1861, 'are displaced, but not removed'.

Already during the 1840s there was a sharp contrast in building densities in different parts of London – the word 'overcrowding' was first used in the 1840s. Social statisticians, whose numbers were increasing, were interested in relating such differences to other social indicators like those of sickness and crime. There was a network of private schools, and schools managed by religious denominations, but no national educational system until after 1870.

Meanwhile, public health arrangements, like housing, remained unsatisfactory. In the words of a recent historian, London was 'like a polluted sponge, a honeycomb of cesspools and wells, water supply taken from the rivers which were used as drains, perpetual fever haunting the slums, and thousands dying in successive epidemics of cholera'. The first 'visitation' of cholera to London had been in 1831 and there was a further epidemic in 1849, the year Marx arrived. Yet even more serious in their effects than cholera were less dramatic diseases like typhus. There was no accident in the fact that the highest London death rates were in Holborn, Shoreditch and Bethnal Green, the older, poorer districts. Nor was it any consolation that London was appreciably healthier than most European cities, and that the 'sanitary idea' had more disciples in London than socialism.

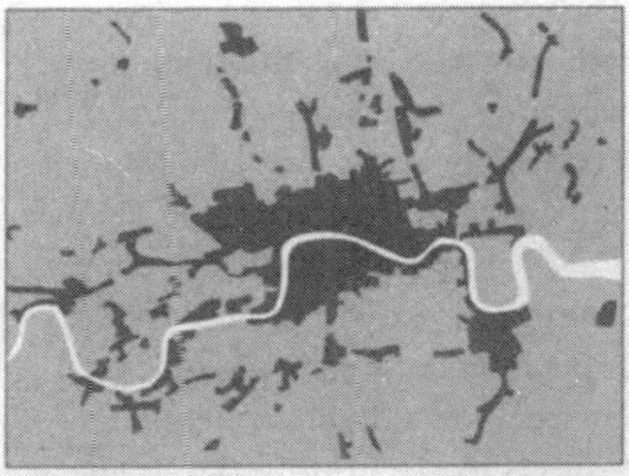
London at the end of the eighteenth century

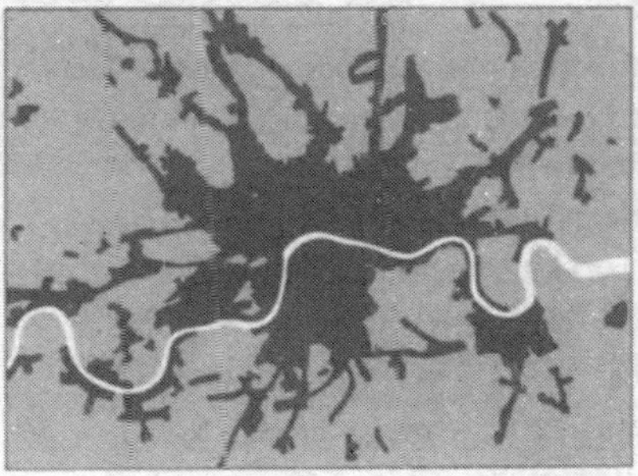
London in the 1830s

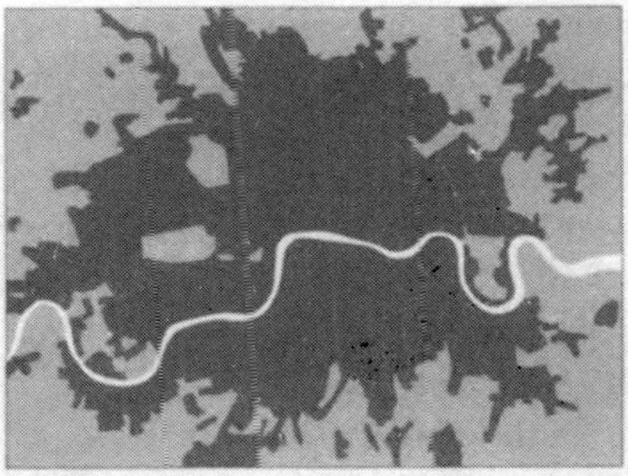
London in the 1870s

It was not until six years after Marx arrived that the Metropolitan Board of Works was created, in 1855. It set about at once to devise a system of sewerage 'which should prevent all or any part of the sewage within the Metropolis from passing into the

Thames in or near the Metropolis', and later on turned its attention to the widening of old streets and the making of new ones, the building of embankments to contain the Thames and the inspection of the gas supply. Slum clearance was more a by-product of these sanitary and environmental improvements and projects than a priority, but its effects were to be socially striking. London became more socially segregated, with the purpose-built single class streets that became characteristic of late-Victorian London.

The suburb which grew fastest in the late Victorian years was Camberwell: indeed, its population increased seven times between 1837 and 1901. It was a suburb for the respectable, among them the growing numbers of clerks who formed an increasingly important element in the changing labour force. Already in the 1840s it had many fine houses, but in the next decades housing standards were to become more limited and uniform, until ultimately Camberwell became a place of standard two-storey brick terraces.

In the late-nineteenth century, London was to play an important part in the history of British socialism. During the late 1830s and early 1840s, however, it seemed in this respect to be lagging behind the industrial north, particularly during the early years of Chartism. Engels met some Chartists in Manchester and Bradford. They included the editor of the pioneering Chartist newspaper, *The Northern Star*, George Julian Harney (1817-1897).

Following the publication of the Charter in May 1838, it was largely the provincial Chartists who organised the world's first large scale working-class movement to secure their still famous 'six points' – votes for all; secret voting; annual parliaments; paid MPs; an end to the then required property-owning qualifications for MPs; and the abolition of corrupt constituencies. 'The worst mistake the Chartist leaders made', wrote H.M. Hyndman, the socialist leader (who was influenced by Marx), 'was that they neglected London until too late.' Hyndman's statement was exaggerated in relation to the whole history of Chartism, however, for although London was relatively inactive at the beginning of the Chartist story in 1838-9, it was always a major centre of active working-class politics.

The National Union of the Working Classes had been founded in London in 1831, and there were many meetings and demonstrations, for example the huge Coldbath Fields gathering in 1833. Around Lincoln's Inn and the Temple there was a collection of radical bookshops, well supported by the public, with plenty of sales for the unstamped *Poor Man's Guardian*, which defied the newspaper tax.

The London Working Men's Association was founded in June

1836 by, among others, William Lovett (1800-1877), a craftsman who had arrived in London from Cornwall. Lovett's object was to 'draw into one bond of union' the 'intelligent … classes'. It was not until 1848 that London came to be at the centre of the Chartist story. There were active revolutionary elements in the London Chartism of that year. Different labour groups, including workers in the 'old trades', rallied to the movement, and some of the most active Chartists turned increasingly to socialist programmes. Nor did Chartist sentiment evaporate after 1848. 'The artisans', wrote Henry Mayhew, author of *London Labour and the London Poor* (1851), 'are almost to a man red-hot proletarians, entertaining violent political opinions.'

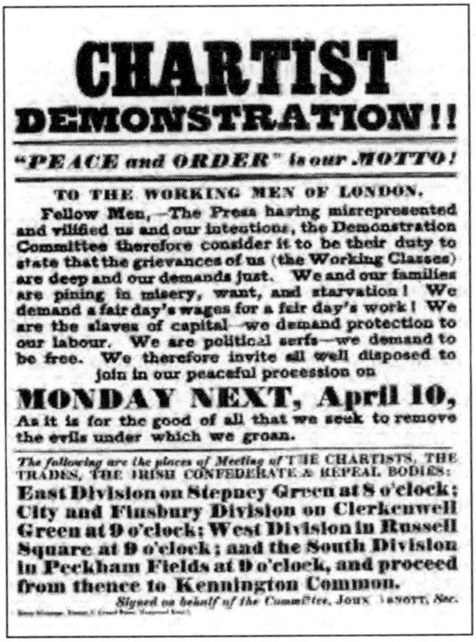
CHARTIST
DEMONSTRATION!!
"PEACE and ORDER" is our *MOTTO!*

TO THE WORKING MEN OF LONDON.

Fellow Men,—The Press having misrepresented and vilified us and our intentions, the Demonstration Committee therefore consider it to be their duty to state that the grievances of us (the Working Classes) are deep and our demands just. We and our families are pining in misery, want, and starvation! We demand a fair day's wages for a fair day's work! We are the slaves of capital—we demand protection to our labour. We are political serfs—we demand to be free. We therefore invite all well disposed to join in our peaceful procession on

MONDAY NEXT, April 10,

As it is for the good of all that we seek to remove the evils under which we groan.

The following are the places of Meeting of THE CHARTISTS, THE TRADES, THE IRISH CONFEDERATE & REPEAL BODIES:

East Division on Stepney Green at 8 o'clock; City and Finsbury Division on Clerkenwell Green at 9 o'clock; West Division in Russell Square at 9 o'clock; and the South Division in Peckham Fields at 9 o'clock, and proceed from thence to Kennington Common.

Signed on behalf of the Committee, JOHN [illegible]NOTT, *Sec.*

There were four elements in the London situation which had held back revolutionary forces in 1848 – a time when revolution was sweeping Europe. First, the propertied London middle classes were strong and in critical situations rallied to the cause of law and order. Second, many radicals were not revolutionaries. They were, for various reasons, unwilling to use physical force. Third, London workers were better paid than workers in the provinces, a fact of great importance in 1838, when the Chartists were stronger in the capital than they were outside, and significant even ten years later when there was obvious distress in the capital and serious unemployment. Fourth, the well-organised Metropolitan police provided a readily available non-military form of control. The force had been founded in 1829 and was able to penetrate the movement through spies and informers.

When the Chartists demonstrated in 1848 at the famous Kennington common meeting, south of the river, on 10 April, hoping to present a petition to Parliament, the forces of law and order were well prepared, and the Duke of Wellington, hero of the Battle of Waterloo, was able to direct them efficiently. Their strongest forces were positioned at Blackfriars Bridge, the Chartists' proposed point for crossing the Thames. Four hundred Metropolitan Police were there, forty of them on horseback.

Marx in London, c. early August 1875

Marx as patriarch. Seated in an ornate chair, with his monocle, and right-hand driven firmly into his formal suit jacket, this is, perhaps, the seminal image of Marx as revolutionary and philosopher.

Earlier assembly points for organised labour in London had been closer to the working-class districts of London – Copenhagen Fields in Islington, for example – but this had largely been built up by 1848, while Hyde Park and Trafalgar Square were too far away for most demonstrators; the disturbances there belong to a later generation.

The revolutionary danger in London after Kennington Common came not from open assemblies but from secret groups. But Marx did not arrive in a city on the eve of revolution. For while it had known great excitements in 1848, thereafter it saw even its reform movements divide, collapse or peter out rather than be suppressed by force. After 1850 Marx would have been for most of the time more conscious of the wealth and power of London than of its revolutionary potential. There was a renewal of prosperity after the financial crisis of 1847 and the unemployment and hunger of 1848, and Engels himself wrote later that by the end of 1850 'anyone who had eyes to see – and was prepared to use them – was bound to appreciate that the storms of revolution were subsiding'.

Within three years of Kennington Common, immense crowds were to mass in London, not for political demonstrations but to quietly look round the great International Exhibition, in the newly built Crystal Palace in Hyde Park. There was more pride in industrial achievements than fear of social breakdown.

3. Life before London

Marx was one of nine children, although only five of them survived into adult life, and he was the only boy to do so. Both his parents came from an orthodox Jewish background, but his father Heinrich had taken full advantage of the greater freedom allowed to Jews during French rule in Trier from 1803 to 1813, to rise to a highly-respected position as a lawyer by the time Karl was born. However, he turned his back on his Jewish heritage after the French left, and was baptised a Lutheran. This meant that Marx himself grew up outside the Jewish community. Moreover, the Lutherans were themselves a minority within Roman Catholic Trier.

Marx's Birthplace: Bruckenstrasse, Trier

The house was built in 1727, and rented by Heinrich Marx in April 1818. Karl was born in the house a month later. The Marx family did not, however, stay long. In October 1819, they moved to a smaller house in the neighbouring Simeonstrasse. Today Marx's birthplace houses a museum and research centre dedicated to his life and work.

Karl was quite fond of his older sister Sophie, but does not seem to have been particularly close to his mother Henrietta, particularly later in life. Through his mother's family, however, he was to have an intriguing connection with the modern capitalist world. His uncle, Lion Philips – from whom Marx would try, throughout his life, to borrow money – was a banker at Zaltbommel in Holland. Marx would regularly visit him, and his cousins Gerard and Anton Philips, who were to go on, in 1891, to found what has now become Philips Electrical Industries in Eindhoven. When descendants of the two families met on one occasion, it is said that the Philips branch quipped to the Marx branch: 'You talked about Capital, whilst we made it!'

Marx had a warm, affectionate relationship with his father, who was a well-educated man with a keen interest in French rationalist philosophy. Another formative influence in his teenage years was a great friend of the family Baron von Westphalen, a liberal, intelligent man with strong romantic leanings. Von Westphalen encouraged the young Karl to read widely and lent him books, and spent much time discussing ideas with a young man he found bright and lively.

At the age of seventeen, after graduating from his secondary school eighth in a class of thirty-two, Marx entered Bonn University as a student of Law. He quickly threw himself into student life, forgetting to write home, writing Byronic poems instead, accumulating debts, and sometimes getting drunk. The upshot was that, after one year at Bonn, his father decided he should transfer to Berlin University, where he hoped there would be a more

The Young Marx, at the White Horse Inn, Godesberg, 1836

This idealised image, by the Soviet artist I. Grinshtein, is based upon a small sketch of Marx among his fellow students at the Tavern Club. Even this university fraternity was a hub of politics. The young liberals and radicals of Trier gravitated towards it, and its members came under frequent attacks from the aristocratic 'Borussia Korps'. Marx, himself, was challenged to a duel, in June 1836, and was lucky to escape with a scar across his left brow.

The Secondary School in Trier, which Marx attended from October 1830 to September 1835

During his time there, Marx was fortunate to benefit from the enlightened teaching of his headmaster, Johann Wyttenbach (1767-1848) who did much to shape his studies and outlook on the world.

sober, studious atmosphere. There was, however, a problem. Before starting his studies at Berlin, Marx had fallen in love with Baron von Westphalen's daughter, Jenny, a beautiful and charming girl who had many suitors in Trier. She was twenty-two, but Marx was only eighteen, and there was a marked difference in their social status, since Jenny's grandmother was a Scottish noblewoman descended from the Dukes of Argyll. Nonetheless, Karl and Jenny overcame family opposition on both sides and their engagement was approved before Karl left the Rhineland, and his fiancée travelled to Berlin.

Berlin, before the revolutions of 1848, was a capital city with 400,000 inhabitants. It had a tense feeling about it, perhaps because, whilst being the seat of Prussian bureaucratic rule, it was also a magnet for German radical intellectuals. The great German philosopher Hegel had taught there from 1818 to 1831, and some of his pupils had been inspired to draw radical conclusions from what he had written. Marx felt the excitement, particularly in the Doctors' Club, where 'Young

Hegelian' ideas of a radical kind were freely discussed. To the dismay of his father, who had wished him to study Law, he found himself increasing drawn towards the study of philosophy. He gradually established a reputation among the radical intellectuals for his wit, erudition and firm stance on philosophical issues. Consequently, in 1841 Marx graduated as a Doctor of Philosophy; his thesis on Ancient Greek philosophy had contemporary significance and he had high hopes of a rewarding academic career.

Jenny von Westphalen, Marx's future wife as a young girl, c.1830s

Despite the hardships of her married life, Jenny never faltered in her devotion to her husband. Engels later paid her the following warm tribute: 'If ever woman found her highest happiness in rendering others happy, that woman was she'.

When this did not materialise and his patrons failed him, he turned to journalism as a means of earning his living. He moved back to the Rhineland, where he began to contribute to the *Rheinische Zeitung*, a progressive journal, published in Cologne. Within ten months, in October 1842, he was made editor. His leaders and articles were radical and uncompromising, but somehow they evaded the censor, until the circulation of the journal rose and the Prussian Government were forced to take notice of its powerful polemics. Finally, after a particularly bitter attack on the Russian Tsar Nicholas I, the newspaper was suppressed in March 1843.

Marx was still only twenty-four, but he decided that if he wanted to write about the things in which he believed he would have to leave Germany. Before doing so, he married Jenny at the Evangelical Church in Trier in June 1843. They honeymooned in Switzerland and set up home in Paris, which had been suggested as a destination by Arnold Ruge, the leader of the Young Hegelians, who was to be described later by Marx as the 'Confucius of the émigrés'. On their arrival in Paris in October of 1843, the Marxes lodged at 23 rue Vaneau. By then Jenny was four months pregnant with their first child, also to be called Jenny.

The rue Vaneau was in St. Germain on the Left Bank, close to the govern-

Marx's lodgings in Paris, at 38 rue Vaneau, where he lived from 1843-45

ment offices along the Quai d'Orsay, and there were many other German emigrants living in the area. Here they set up a primitive attempt at a commune with the families of Ruge – with whom Marx was collaborating as joint editor of the *Deutsche-Französiche Jahrbücher* – and Germain Mauer, another German socialist émigré. The arrangement did not please the newly married Jenny and within a fortnight they had moved out, eventually to settle at number 38 rue Vaneau. The façade of the house still stands today, although, with an irony that applies to so many of the old haunts of the revolutionaries, the interior has been stripped out and converted into a block of luxury apartments. Karl and Jenny were to stay in the rue Vaneau until leaving for Brussels in February 1845.

Marx spent long nights in Paris avidly reading books on economics, politics and philosophy and writing manuscripts which were not to be published until almost half a century after his death. Above all, he read as much as he could on the French Revolution of 1789, seeking to discover why it had 'failed' and how it could be replicated and bettered. Marx was made welcome in fashionable Paris 'salons', and here he met the German romantic poet Heinrich Heine (1797-1856), whose works he much admired, and the Russian revolutionary Mikhail Bakunin (1814-1876), who was later to join the First International, only to be expelled by Marx after bitter and protracted conflicts.

The hope of France, Marx came to argue, did not depend on the talkers in the salons, but on the proletariat in the streets; he argued that manual workers were exploited by their masters. Politics had an economic and social base, for 'the course of world history was determined by definite laws and in any society the social and political stature of the state was determined by the way in which goods were produced'. He wrote that 'communists' should be 'the first to stress social questions'. Given these convictions, he came into contact with the League of the Just (*Bund der Gerichten*), a secret society founded in 1836. He persuaded the leadership to alter its programme so that within a few years it was a socialist body, later to be renamed the Communist League. At the same time, he was supporting himself and Jenny by writing articles for journals published in Paris for German distribution, such as *Vorwarts* and the *Deutsche-Französische Jahrbücher* (of which only one issue was ever produced).

It was through such journalism that he was drawn into close connection with Frederick Engels (1820-1895). The two men had first met in Cologne in November 1842, but it was not until Engels wrote 'Outline of a Critique of Political Economy' for the *Jahrbucher* that the two men realised, in Paris during the summer of 1844, how much they had in common. They were to go on to collaborate in writing *The Holy Family* in 1845 (an attack, mainly written by Marx, on some of the leading Young Hegelians) and *The German Ideology*, written in the spring of 1846. By then, the Prussians had successfully put pressure on the French government of King Louis Philippe to suppress the German journals published in Paris. Marx and other revolutionaries had been expelled from France in February 1845. Karl and Jenny moved to Brussels, where industrialisation was more advanced than France and where there was considerable socialist ferment. Two children were born to them there: Laura in 1846 and Edgar in 1847.

Engels joined the Marxes in the spring of 1845, and in the summer they were living next door to each other at numbers 5 and 7 rue de l' Alliance.

The houses, numbers 5-7, on the Rue de l' Alliance, Brussels, occupied by Marx and Engels

Marx and his growing family occupied no.5 from May 1845 to May 1846, while Engels stayed on in no.7 until June 1846. Despite police surveillance, these houses became the favourite meeting places for exiled revolutionaries and Belgian democrats.

They spent their time arguing with other socialists and in the process clarifying their own thinking. They were drawn increasingly into a web of revolutionary activity through the Communist Correspondence Committee, which they set up in 1846. The German Workers' Association in Brussels was part of the network, and so, too, from June 1846, was the German Workers' Education Society in London.

Short visits to London, first by Engels in June 1847, and later by Marx and Engels in November 1847, involved what Engels called 'decisive' discussions with the Communist League. While in London they also attended a meeting of the Fraternal Democrats, on the anniversary of the Polish rising of 1830, and they addressed a meeting of the German Workers' Education Society. The slogan of the Communist League, which claimed a membership of five hundred, had been changed at the insistence of Engels from 'All men are brothers' to 'Workers of all countries unite', in line with their increasingly sharp assault on all older utopian, or rival, versions of socialism. There were a lot of men, Marx gruffly observed, whose brother he certainly did not wish to be! Their by now well-articulated philosophy of action rested not on 'sentiment', or simple 'idealism', but upon a 'scientific' conclusion that 'the capitalist mode of production' would 'inevitably' collapse. Indeed, they felt, amid worsening living conditions for the rapidly expanding working class, that the collapse was 'daily taking place before our eyes'.

At the behest of the Communist League, which was in touch with Paris, Brussels, Switzerland and Sweden, Marx and Engels produced the *Communist Manifesto* of 1848, which appeared in German in February 1848 on the eve of Europe's great chain of revolutions. This was to remain a landmark document for future revolutionaries throughout the world. Its appeal lay in both its dazzling language and its content. It ranged widely over the past, summarised the present, and peered into the future, claiming boldly that revolution was bound to come. It proposed a redistribution of wealth, to be achieved through the introduction of income tax; the abolition of the great landed estates; free education; and the nationalisation of industry. Its proposals – which in themselves were revolutionary enough – were underpinned by a radical and wholly new vision of what was to come. The prosperity and power of the middle class, who had achieved unprecedented control over the forces of production, were doomed to disappear. In its rise to dominance, the bourgeoisie had forged the very weapons that would bring about its demise – the new proletariat – which had become a revolutionary class, the agent of change, with nothing to lose but its chains.

Marx and Engels in the print shop of the *Neue Rheinische Zeitung*, 1848

This heroic painting, done by Yuri Sapiro in 1961, conveys something of the excitement and drama experienced by Marx and Engels during the 'Year of Revolutions'. As Marx checks the copy, fresh from the press, Engels, and Georg Weerth (1822-1856) and Wilhelm Wolff (1809-1864), their fellow members of the editorial board, stand in attendance, with a stack of muskets close at hand.

There was, of course, no revolution in England in 1848; and the *Manifesto* made very little impact in Britain, having to wait two years before it was translated into English (when it was published in the *Red Republican*, a new periodical edited by prominent Chartist George Julian Harney). By then, however, revolutionary Europe had given way to reaction. One by one the insurrections that had taken fire in France, Austro-Hungary, Poland, Prussia and the states of Southern Germany, were snuffed out by professionalised armies and storms of grapeshot.

Marx was expelled from Brussels on 4 March 1848, with so little warning that the family had to leave their silver plate and best linen behind. They then spent a month in revolutionary Paris (from where he watched the Communist League disintegrate) before moving to Cologne, where Marx edited the *Neue Rheinische Zeitung*. There he survived a number of writs, and his newspaper – which advocated an armed uprising –

suffered from a period of suspension. Marx found it increasingly difficult to find the necessary funds to keep it afloat, and was increasingly worried about the counter-revolutionary course of events in Germany and France. Finally, in May 1849, he was served with notice of expulsion. His newspaper managed to last for three more days, and the last issue was printed in bright red ink. With justifiable bravado, Engels recalled that: 'wonder was expressed that we carried on our activities so unconcernedly within a Prussian fortress of the first rank, in the face of a garrison of 8,000 troops and in the face of a guardhouse; but, on account of the eight rifles and bayonets and 250 live cartridges in the editorial room, and the red Jacobin caps of the compositors, our house was reckoned by the officers also as a fortress which was not to be taken by a mere *coup de main*'.

From Cologne Marx moved across Germany (at Frankfurt more of the family silver was pawned), before finding temporary refuge back in Paris. He arrived in London in the late summer, spending his first nights in Camberwell. His wife and three children followed him three weeks later. England, which had escaped the reaction as well as the revolution, then became his home for the rest of his life

The Marx's first family home in London was in one of the more fashionable parts of the city – even then – **4 Anderson Street,** just off the King's Road in Chelsea. It was there that a

Marx's first London home: 4 Anderson Street, Chelsea

Marx was 31 years old when, in August 1849, he took up residence in Chelsea. He expected that his stay would be a short one, and that he would be quickly called back to France or Germany to assist in further revolutionary outbreaks. However, the planned revolutions failed to materialise and Marx quickly ran out of money and was forcibly ejected, in April 1850, from this swish neighbourhood.

fourth child, Henry, was born, on Guy Fawkes Night 1849; the boy was nicknamed 'Guido', in honour of the man who had tried to blow up Parliament. Life in Chelsea proved comfortable, at least for a while, but the rent, £6 a month, was high. Not surprisingly, with no money coming

The German Hotel, Leicester Street

For many years the building has been home to the famous fish restaurant, Manzi's. However, the business closed in the summer of 2006 and the premises are currently vacant, awaiting redevelopment. It is to be hoped that, in its plans, Westminster City Council will seek to respect the building's integrity and historic past.

Plaque on the front of the former German Hotel, Leicester Street, commemorating the visit to London of Johann Strauss, the elder

The German Hotel was home to many refugees, fleeing repression after the collapse of the revolutionary movements across Europe in 1848. It is, therefore, ironic that neither their sacrifice nor that of Marx are today recorded in the building. Rather, it is Johann Strauss, who supported the forces of monarchy and reaction, who is honoured. Indeed, his 'Radetzky March' commemorated the actions of the Austro-Hungarian general who ruthlessly put down the revolutionary movement. It is interesting to note, however, that Strauss's own son opposed his father's ideas and served on the barricades, in Vienna, alongside the revolutionaries.

in, the Marxes very quickly got into debt. After the local tradesmen had pressed for payment of their bills, the bailiffs were called in and seized everything that could be taken, including the baby's cradle and the girls' toys. The whole family was evicted unceremoniously, much to the delight of a watching crowd.

As Jenny described life with the baby at the time:

> you will see that few emigrants, perhaps, have gone through anything like it. As wet-nurses here are too expensive I decided to feed my child myself in spite of continual terrible pains in the breast and back. But the poor little angel drank in so much worry and hushed-up anxiety that he was always poorly and suffered horribly day and night. Since he came into the world he has not slept a single night, two or three hours at the most and that rarely.

As for the eviction:

> there were two or three hundred persons loitering around our door – the whole Chelsea mob. The beds were brought in again – they could not be delivered to the buyer until after sunrise next day. When we had sold all our possessions we were in a position to pay what we owed to the last farthing. I went with my little darlings to the two small rooms we are now occupying in the **German Hotel**, 1 Leicester St., Leicester Square. There for £5 per week we were given a humane reception.

The German Hotel was a transit camp for many political refugees who had fled from failed revolutionary upheavals in continental Europe. But the Marxes did not stay there long. They had to find even more money than in Chelsea for their accommodation, and, in Jenny's simple words: 'one morning our host refused to serve us our breakfast and we were forced to look for other lodgings'.

How to get there

Anderson Street, SW3

By underground to Sloane Square Station
(District and Circle Lines)
By bus – routes 11, 19, 22, 137 & C2

Leicester Street, WC2

By underground to Leicester Square Station
(Piccadilly and Northern Lines)
By bus – routes 3, 6, 9, 11, 12, 13, 15, 23, 24, 53, 77A, 88, 91, 139 & 159

4. Exiles and revolutionaries

The London of the 1840s, like Paris, included a significant exile and revolutionary population both before and after the revolutions of 1848. Exiles and revolutionaries could find a greater freedom in London after 1851, because France became a Napoleonic Empire once again, after the demise of the short-lived republic. And even during the republic, there were so many shifts of fortune – and attitudes towards exiles and revolutionaries – that the security and relative freedom of London was much prized. A third capital city, Brussels, had some of the advantages of both London and Paris, but it was never a place for a long-term stay. Nor was Switzerland, though it too retained its appeal for revolutionary exiles through into the twentieth century.

Baron Bunsen, the Prussian Ambassador in London, reported in 1851 that there were in the capital at that time about a thousand foreign refugees who belonged to political organisations of one kind and another. The numbers had increased since 1849, when Marx arrived permanently in London, but there were already two hundred and fifty members of the German Workers' Education Society in London as early as 1846, and Karl Schapper, its organiser, wrote to Marx then about the Society's activities (see pp37, 39). They were concentrated in the London that Marx was to come to know well, and rented a hall in Drury Lane. Schapper also eagerly reported that the Society was 'trying to get into Whitechapel, where there are thousands of Germans', and a branch there had at last been founded.

The German Workers' Education Society, founded in 1840 in **Great Windmill Street** on the edge of Soho, not far from Piccadilly Circus, was not a revolutionary group. It still kept the slogan that 'all men were brothers'. In 1847 it included in its ranks – according to Schapper's information – forty Scandinavians, twenty Hungarians, 'and in addition Poles, Russians, Italians, Swiss, Belgians, French, English, etc'.

Broadly speaking, there were several more or less distinct and coherent national groups among the exiles and revolutionaries in London, with nationalism a lively and influential ideology amongst them. This was particularly true for the Poles, whose nation had been suppressed, and the Italians, whose nation had still not been united. The Italians were, for the most part, strongly opposed to

The Red Lion, Great Windmill Street, Soho

Marx visited London in 1847, in order to attend the Second Congress of the Communist League for which he and Friedrich Engels were commissioned to draw up the Communist Manifesto. The Congress, which lasted from 29 November to 8 December, was held in the hall of the German Workers' Education Society in the upper part of the Red Lion public house. In 1850-51, Marx gave a course on economics in the building. The pub closed in the autumn of 2006, and is currently being redeveloped as London rates continue to soar and the face of the city is continually refashioned.

The White Hart Inn, Drury Lane

During his stay in London, in 1847, Marx also addressed a meeting of the German Workers' Education Society in an upstairs room at the White Hart. Although much modified, there has been an inn, continuously, on this site since 1216.

Socialism. The 'Young Italy' movement, led by Giuseppe Mazzini (1805-1872), was liberal, and relied, though not exclusively, on strong middle-class support. Mazzini was very popular in England, but Marx was scathing in his criticism of the European Central Democratic Committee that he founded in 1850, in an attempt to foster unity among refugees from different countries.

Indeed, it could be argued that Marx's failure to account for the power of nationalism to cut across the boundaries of class was a major flaw in his theoretical work.

Yet the claims of different nations, and of humanity as a whole, were still taken to be complementary by most, so that there was always a great deal of international activity, especially on national anniversary days. Moreover, since the forces of order against which the exiles were in revolt were thought, usually correctly, to be in alliance with each other across the borders of states (some of which, like the Hapsburg Empire, were multi- and anti-national), it seemed to be a duty of the exiles and revolutionaries as a whole to work against common enemies. This was true both before the revolutionary uprisings of 1848 began, and after 1849 when the European counter-revolution was consolidated. The part played by Russian armies in the process of consolidation had increased hostility towards the Russian Empire, so that Russian exiles and revolutionaries, though themselves fleeing Tsarist autocracy, were usually the least welcome people in the exile and revolutionary groups.

The Poles were conspicuous in agitation and organisation from the start, and received a warm welcome from the English Chartists, notably George Julian Harney. Harney had also met Engels in 1843 (see p18), at the office of the Chartist newspaper *The Northern Star* in Leeds (its office was later moved to Great Windmill Street in London), and commissioned from him two long articles on European Socialism. Marx was to break with Harney in 1851, calling him 'our ex-Dear' friend, but Engels remained in intermittent contact with him, and visited him in 1892 when he was old and ill.

William Lovett was a very different kind of 'moral force' Chartist, but he was just as internationalist in outlook as Harney, and in 1844 formed the first international society in London, the Democratic Friends of All Nations. By then he had become a close friend of Giuseppe Mazzini, supporting him strongly after the British Government had intercepted his mail. The new society, however, was not a success; it was not sufficiently militant to appeal to most exiles. A more successful organisation, the Fraternal Democrats, was launched by Harney in September 1845, at a banquet to celebrate the French Republican

Constitution of 1792. It included Frenchmen, Germans, Poles – who had their own democratic society – Swiss, Hungarians and one Turkish democrat, who sang Turkish songs to the assembled guests at the founding banquet.

Not all exiles and revolutionaries in London were convinced by Harney's left-wing Chartism. Indeed, social differences between exiles and revolutionaries usually counted for more than national differences, then and later; and there were bitter divisions amongst the London Poles following the Cracow uprising in 1846. Yet the German groups, in particular, moved further to the left between 1847 and 1849 and were ready to welcome Marx when he arrived in London. By occupation most of them were artisans. For example, Karl Schapper was a compositor, Joseph Moll a watchmaker, Heinrich Bauer a shoemaker. A fourth activist who was to play an important part in the future Marx story was Johann Georg Eccarius (1818-1889), a tailor.

Schapper, who became German secretary of the Fraternal Democrats, had been an exile in Paris before he came to London, and had participated, like Moll and Bauer, in the abortive Paris insurrection of 1839. They were all members of the League of the Just, and were already seasoned professional revolutionaries. For example Schapper had participated in an attack on a Frankfurt guardhouse in 1833, and had joined an abortive Mazzini expedition to Savoy in 1836.

The German Workers' Education Society provided a cover for the activities of the League of the Just, but it had a vigorous social and cultural life of its own – and an offshoot, the Sunday Club, which attracted even the non-politically minded. In his letter to Marx in 1846, Schapper not only outlined the way the Education Society worked, but caught its style and mood:

> Our Society numbers about 250 members. We meet three times a week. On Tuesdays there are alternately reports on current politics and discussions: one Tuesday is devoted to Feuerbach's *Religion of the Future*, which we are discussing paragraph by paragraph, and the next to questions raised by members of the Society themselves. The latest question which we discussed was the upbringing of youth in a Communist State. Our problem is to give all members of the Society an opportunity to raise for discussion any question concerning our principles, which is not yet clear to them, in this way seeking complete clarity. Saturday evening is devoted to singing, music, recitations and reading interesting newspaper articles; on Sunday lectures are given on ancient and modern history, geography, astronomy, etc, and then questions of the present position of the workers and their attitude to the

Engels directing the artillery at Elberfeld, May 1849

While others talked of revolution, Engels transformed the appearance of his home town, ringing it with deep entrenchments and formidable bastions. One Sunday morning, the story goes, Engels – attired in the blood red sash of a revolutionary – met on the town bridge his father – clad in his best attire, ready for church. What they said to each other is not recorded, and may not even have been overheard, but as a sign of old and new worlds colliding and of family relations being torn asunder by sudden revolutionary upheavals, there can be few more dramatic and instructive.

The Town Hall of Wupperthal-Elberfeld, c.1850

It was here, on 11 May 1849, that Engels presented himself at the headquarters of the local revolutionary movement and was employed as a military specialist, to assist in the rising. The Town Hall was draped in the red-black-gold colours of the bourgeoisie revolution but it was Engels' involvement in raising the red banners, of working class insurrection, across the town that led to his rapid dismissal after less than a week of service.

> bourgeoisie are discussed in turn … On Mondays the French Society meets, at which the system of Communism is discussed. True, it still looks very like Republicanism, but nevertheless we learn something there, and have the opportunity to acquaint Frenchmen with our ideas.
>
> Once a fortnight we meet jointly with the English (the "Fraternal Democrats"), and I can say that these meetings have already been very valuable for both sides … On Wednesday evenings there are singing lessons, on Thursdays language and drawing lessons, on Fridays dancing lessons. Our library numbers about 500 books: in addition, we have geographical and astronomical globes, maps, and German, French, English and Scandinavian newspapers. We keep up good connections in France, Switzerland, Scandinavia, Hungary, Germany, America and other countries where there are former members of our Society; they inform us from time to time of the successes of the movement in their countries.

Schapper's letter was sent to Marx in Marx's capacity as organiser of the Communist Correspondence Committee, set up in Brussels, where Marx and Engels were in exile in 1845. By that time, they had already reached the conclusion stated clearly by Marx in the spring of 1845 – in his theses on Ludwig Feuerbach (1804-1872), the German materialist philosopher – that 'the philosophers have only *interpreted* the world in various ways. The *point however is to change it*'. They also visited England together during the summer of 1845, when Engels took Marx to Manchester to show him not only what Europe's major industrial city was liked but also the famous Chetham's Library, which included a sizeable collection of works by British economists.

When Marx settled in London four years later, he had established the kernel of his political and philosophical thought: that theory and practice could not be separated; that humanity was the basic factor in society; and that the proletariat, forged in the fires of the Industrial Revolution, was the determining force which would bring about the fundamental changes required for the creation of a more equitable society. With a support network of other political exiles, and the opportunity to witness the unprecedented pace of economic change in England at first hand, Marx was in a uniquely advantageous position to analyse the development of capitalist society, and to help shape the growth of the working class movement that was arising in opposition to it.

When Marx began his life in London, he expected further revolutionary outbreaks across Europe. As he struggled to find a home for his family in the city, he saw it as only a temporary refuge before returning to the fray. Perhaps fortunately, he had no way of knowing that the ebb tide of revolution, which had washed him up onto English shores, would not turn again for more than twenty years to come.

How to get there

The Red Lion, Great Windmill Street, Soho, W1

By underground to Piccadilly Circus (Piccadilly Line)

By bus – routes 3, 6, 9, 12, 13, 14, 15, 19, 22, 23, 38, 53, 88, 94, 139, 159

(for map see p49)

5. Soho years

The first real home in Soho for the Marx family was not far from the German Hotel, at **64 Dean Street**. 'We found two rooms in the house of a Jewish lace dealer', Jenny wrote, 'and spent a miserable summer there with our four children'. The original house no longer exists, and they stayed there only from 8 May to 2 December 1850.

Their home for the next six years was to be three rooms in the same street, at the top floor of number **28 Dean Street**. Today the house bears a blue memorial plaque affixed by the Greater London Council in the 1970s, with the incorrect inscription: 'Karl Marx, 1818-1883, lived here 1851-1856' (in fact he lived there from 1850). This is the only place where Marx's thirty-four years in England are thus commemorated.

Dean Street, as it was in the late nineteenth century

The commemorative GLC Blue Plaque – complete with the wrong dates! – on the front of 28 Dean Street.

Whilst living here, Marx wrote the greater part of the first volume of Capital. His daughter, Franziska, was born here in 1851.

28 Dean Street, the well-known 'Quo Vadis' Restaurant

Marx's name is commemorated over the main entrance, together with the restaurant's former owner, Raffaello Leoni. When a journalist from the Daily Mirror and his counterpart from Pravda toured London, in the 1960s, in search of places where Marx had lived, Leoni was the most welcoming of the, then, owners. 'People come here for good food', he said, 'not to see Karl Marx'. But added on reflection that he'd put up a plaque himself: 'Just send me the dates'.

Marx commodified?

The view down Dean Street today. A vegetarian café chain plays on Marx's work to sell its wares. Inside, customers can choose their veggie burgers from bill boards decorated with pictures of Marx, Lenin, Che Guevara and Ho Chi Minh. Socialist chic sells!

By the time the family moved into their cramped apartment, at the beginning of December 1850, Jenny was pregnant again, and a fifth child, Franziska, was born in March 1851. Their landlord was an Italian-born cook, John Marengo. They also had living with them their faithful maid 'Lenchen', whose real name was Helene Demuth (1823-1890), together with an English nurse for Jenny's confinement. Shortly after their arrival, Marx was recorded by the Census Enumerator of 1851 as: 'Charles Mark, Doctor (Philosophical Author)'.

Cosmopolitan Soho was already a favourite district for French, Italians, Swiss, Germans and others. The other occupants of number 28 in 1851, the year of the Great Exhibition, were an Italian-born confectioner and a 'teacher of languages', Morgan Kavanagh, who sub-let his part of the house to Marx.

Number 28 is a typical narrow-fronted Georgian house, simple but elegant, dating from 1734. There are many such houses in London, and, although the Victorians were reacting against the formal Georgian style, they were remarkably flexible in their patterns of use. Georgian houses could easily be adapted for other uses besides private residences, and they could be turned into hotels, offices and shops. The houses of Dean Street and some of the neighbouring streets were among the most beautiful in London, but they lacked most of the conveniences of a later generation.

Helene Demuth, 'Lenchen'

In the spring of 1845, Jenny Marx's mother – Caroline von Westphalen – packed off a young serving maid to help her daughter. Helene took over the management of the household and devoted herself to the Marx family, becoming a trusted friend and confidant.

There would have been a primitive water closet, however, albeit a communal one on the ground floor, and not flushed from the mains water supply. Water came into the house in iron pipes, so that the family was spared the indignity of having to go to the nearest public pump for fresh water, but the pressure would only bring it up to a height of ten feet above ground. Life must have been hard for Lenchen, who had to fetch the water for the washing and cooking and laundry from the ground floor.

Much of old Soho remains today. It is a district of narrow byways, with a crowded outdoor market in Berwick Street. The important 'boundary streets' were built some time after the Marxes moved out, however: Shaftesbury Avenue from 1877 to 1886, and Charing Cross Road in 1887; and these sliced through some of the worst slums. The neighbourhood during the 1850s was noisy, bustling and cheerful, perhaps more so than today, when it is largely given over to food, drink, sex and the media industry. Indeed, traditionally occupied as it was by small craftsmen, many of them foreigners, it must have seemed very much like home to countless political exiles over the years, squalid though corners of it were. Despite his own problems, Marx served on a relief committee to help penniless refugees.

The Marx family was especially cramped because Karl needed one of the three rooms for his study. Having come to realise that the chances of imminent revolution were receding, he busied himself here in his self-appointed life's task – interpreting the world and trying to change it for the better.

At first he had put his hopes in a new body, the Universal Society of Revolutionary Communists, founded in April 1850, but this soon collapsed, as did the Communist League itself. It had split after he and Engels could no longer control it. Thereafter, he was to concentrate on study – he secured a ticket for the British Museum Reading Room in June 1850 – and on holding court to visiting European revolutionaries and the occasional Prussian police agent. Marx gave his advice on revolutionary strategy to everyone whom he found interesting, including some visitors who actually requested it. Here too he wrote at his desk, seeking to order and systematise as well as to extend his knowledge of economics and politics. Before 1850 was over, he had edited, from a distance, five numbers of the *Neue Rheinische Zeitung*.

A Prussian police agent has left a report of their home life in Dean Street which carries the ring of truth:

> As father and husband, Marx, in spite of his wild and restless character, is the gentlest and mildest of men. Marx lives in one of the worst, therefore one of the cheapest, quarters of London. He occupies two rooms [the servants had the third]. The one looking out on the street is the parlour and the bedroom is at the back. In the whole apartment there is not one clean and solid piece of furniture. A seller of second-hand goods would be ashamed to give away such a remarkable collection of odds and ends.
>
> When you enter Marx's room smoke and tobacco fumes make your eyes water so much that for a moment you seem to be groping about in a cavern, but gradually, as you grow accustomed to the fog, you

> can make out certain objects which distinguish themselves from the surrounding haze. Everything is dirty, and covered with dust, so that to sit down becomes a thoroughly dangerous business. Here is a chair with only three legs, on another the children are playing at cooking – this chair happens to have four legs. This is the one which is offered to the visitor, but the children's cooking has not been wiped away; and if you sit down, you risk a pair of trousers.

Marx's working routine was, to say the least, flexible, as the same agent witnessed:

> In private life he is an extremely disorderly, cynical human being, and a bad host. He leads a real gypsy existence. Washing, grooming and changing his linen are things he does rarely, and he is often drunk. Though he is often idle for days on end, he will work day and night with tireless endurance when he has a great deal of work to do. He has no fixed times for going to sleep and waking up. He often stays up all night, and then lies down fully clothed on the sofa at midday and sleeps till evening, untroubled by the whole world coming and going through the room.

Marx's only paid employment from 1851 to 1862 was the writing of a regular column on European events for the *New York Daily Tribune*, a popular newspaper with a large circulation, whose editor, Charles Dana, he had met in Cologne. At first, because his command of the English language was as yet imperfect, it was Engels who wrote many of the articles that bore Marx's name. Marx also contributed to the *People's Paper*, produced by the Chartist Ernest Jones (1819-1869), a well-off and well-educated man, who spoke fluent German and, unlike Harney, accepted the main tenets of Marx's political philosophy.

During this period Marx also tried to come to terms with the defeat of the revolutionary movements of 1848-1849 and to suggest new approaches to the struggle. France in the nineteenth century was synonymous with revolution, and he therefore turned his attention to providing an analysis of recent developments there. *The Class Struggles in France* was written in 1850 and examined the economic factors that underpinned both the creation and destruction of the revolution. *The Eighteenth Brumaire of Louis Napoleon*, written in 1852, was perhaps his most brilliant polemical work. In it he charted the rise to power of Louis Napoleon, showing the manner in which appeals to order and the defence of property had effectively disarmed radical sentiment and subverted the republican constitution.

As the spy noted, Karl worked late, smoking many cigars. He often slept much of the day on a sofa. Until Engels came to his aid he was very poor, in 1853 pawning his overcoat twice in the same year. He became keenly conscious of what he called 'the petty, paltry, bourgeois struggle', which he knew was wearing out his wife, and seriously entertained for a time the idea of emigrating to the New World, as so many other German exiles had done. However, he lacked the money to pay the fare across the Atlantic, and he did not know that assisted passages were being offered to political exiles by the British Government. In December 1845 he had given up his Prussian nationality, and he remained stateless for the rest of his life.

The family's support was assured by Engels, who had moved back to Manchester in November 1850 to work as a clerk in his father's cotton firm, at a salary of £200 a year. Engels would have preferred to keep a fine table and a cellar of good wine, but ensured instead that his friend was saved from the harshest extremes of poverty. Karl had helped him in 1848 and 1849: now and for long afterwards he reciprocated. His first gift was £2. Thereafter money often arrived in separate envelopes, for security each containing two halves of different notes. Sometimes, however, there were only stamps. When Marx was not borrowing money for himself – and sometimes even when he was – he would lend it to comrades whose need was even greater than his. Borrowing and lending were a central feature of refugee life. The years in Dean Street were, indeed, shabby and sad, for others beside himself.

Marx certainly learnt how to avoid too great a pressure from his creditors. Thus, when the family doctor pressed for payment of his bill, the whole Marx family retreated for ten weeks to the house of a friend, Peter Imandt, in more salubrious Camberwell, and afterwards Karl hid in Manchester, in Engels's house, for another three months. This was only one of several trips to Manchester, which gave him a glimpse of the world of machinery and steam, of capitalist production in operation. Engels lived permanently in Manchester until 1869, and Marx's

Engels in Manchester, 1856

Engels appears, here, as the prosperous mill owner. Few of his business friends would have guessed at the extent of his revolutionary commitments, or at his unconventional private life, screened by a cloak of 'respectability'.

visits there often lasted for several weeks. Sadly, the last of Engels's houses was demolished in the summer of 1982; and the surviving chimney of the Victoria mill, built by his father's firm in 1837, was reduced to demolition dust in 1988.

Jenny Marx made one lengthy visit home to Trier in 1856 in order to be present at her mother's deathbed. She had visited Germany and Holland two years earlier, and had received a number of legacies in 1855 which enabled her to take back from the pawn shop silver, linen and clothes. One trip, however, to Marx's uncle in Holland, to ask for money, was fruitless.

Three of the Marx children died in Dean Street: Henry, not year one old; the baby girl, Franziska; and Edgar or 'Mouche', who died of consumption aged eight. All of the children had nicknames, as Marx himself did – 'the Moor' on account of his swarthy complexion. Edgar's funeral at the Whitfield Street Tabernacle, at that time just off Tottenham Court Road (it fronts onto it today, having been rebuilt after bombing in the Second World War) was a deeply distressing affair, when Karl had to be forcibly restrained from throwing himself into his son's open grave.

Poverty meant a loss of dignity, felt most by Jenny Marx, who confided to friends in her letters how she would

Beneath the fallen leaf mulch, this little plaque is set into the pavement off Tottenham Court Road, commemorating Marx's son, Henry, who lies buried in an otherwise unmarked grave close by.

Two more of Marx's young children, Edgar and Franziska, are also buried in this paved area, though there is nothing now to record their fates.

The site of the Whitfield Tabernacle

The church, itself, was destroyed by a flying bomb during the Second World War.

A newly erected glass panel, on the site of the Whitfield Tabernacle, records Marx's links with the area around Tottenham Court Road

Facing him is Charles Darwin (1809-1882), whose theory of evolution held similarly revolutionary potential for the Victorian mind. By the end of the nineteenth century Eduard Bernstein would attempt to see politics as an evolutionary science, grafting elements of Darwin's theories ad hoc on to those of Marx.

often lie awake at night, weeping. Her chief duty was as Karl's unpaid secretary and fair copyist (even though her own handwriting and command of English were far from perfect: it was she who prepared the proofs for the printer, since Marx's handwriting was illegible). The cleaning and cooking was done, of course, by Lenchen (her other nickname was 'Nimm'). Lenchen became pregnant at about the same time as Jenny Marx, and gave birth to a male child in June 1851, registered in August as Henry Frederick Demuth. It is widely believed that Marx was the child's father.

Jenny recorded simply in her autobiography that in the early summer of 1851, 'an event occurred that I do not wish to relate here in detail, although it greatly contributed to an increase in our worries, both personal and others'. The event was not mentioned to the Marx children, who learned of the circumstances from Engels long after Marx's death. The baby was packed off at once to foster parents, Engels accepted paternity, and the affair was hushed up. The birth did not, however, mean the end of the family relationship. Nor did Lenchen leave.

The youngest Marx child, Eleanor, was born in January 1855, a few months before Edgar died in Karl's arms. She was described by Wilhelm Liebknecht as 'a merry little thing, as round as a bell and like cream and roses', and she was soon a favourite of the family.

How to get there

Dean Street, Soho, W1

By underground to Tottenham Court Road Station (Northern and Central Lines)

By bus – routes 7, 8, 10, 14, 19, 24, 25, 38, 55, 73, 98 & 242

The Whitfield Tabernacle, Tottenham Court Road, W1

By underground to Goodge Street Station (Northern Line).

By bus – routes 24 & 7

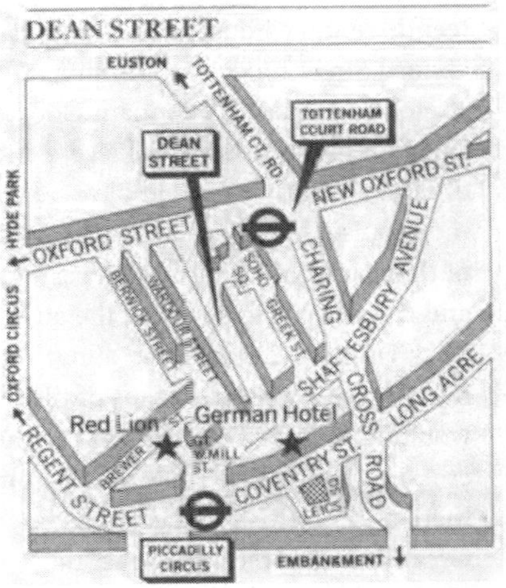

6. Bloomsbury

From Dean Street, Marx had to make only a short journey to work – to the Reading Room of the **British Museum** in Bloomsbury. He could walk up Dean Street to Soho Square and from there into Oxford Street, which was even then an important shopping centre. Although the modern department store had not yet reached London, Marx would have seen the large plate-glass windows that were installed during the 1840s in big, busy shops.

There are few of the early nineteenth-century houses remaining in Oxford Street today and the short stretch of modern Tottenham Court Road on his route also looks very different. But there would have been more noise then than now – the noise of thousands of iron-rimmed carriage- and cartwheels. In summer the air was thick with powdered horse dung, and in rainy weather great heaps of filth would have to be brushed clear of the crossing places. The route today from there to the British Museum, down Great Russell Street, goes past the modern landmarks of the massive concrete YMCA building and the TUC headquarters – with its bronze sculpture of the 'Helping Hand' given by one worker to another.

If any part of London could lay claim to be the 'intellectuals quarter', it was Bloomsbury – although Thomas Carlyle (1795-1881) once caustically remarked that 'there are several persons in a state of imbecility who come to read in the British Museum'. In the twentieth century it was to be associated with the Bloomsbury Group, which included Virginia Woolf, Lytton Strachey and John Maynard Keynes. The massive quintessentially 1930s Senate House building of London University came later. But the Bloomsbury Marx knew was the creation of the seventeenth and eighteenth centuries, and of the development of the Bedford Estate.

After the Restoration of the monarchy in 1660, Bloomsbury Square was laid out, and building started along a quiet country lane to the west of the square, today's Great Russell Street. From here Christopher Wren could look out across open meadows to Highgate. One of the new buildings in Great Russell Street was Montagu House, which was a museum from 1759 onwards, when it also began to house the library of the Kings of England. (The British Museum itself was created by Act of Parliament in 1753.) Montagu House was already providing reading rooms for scholars, but, with the acquisition in 1823 of the vast library that had belonged to King George III, and a large private collection of pictures in the following year, the Trustees started work on a new building – a colossal project which took thirty-four years to complete.

From the time of the passing of the Copyright Acts, the last in 1842, a copy of every book published in Britain had to be deposited with the British Museum Library (now the British Library, which moved to its new, purpose-designed building on Euston Road in 1998). There are now three million books added each year, with more than 150 million volumes already on the shelves. Even during the 1830s there was a growing demand for space for students to consult the books, and the energetic new Keeper of Printed Books, exiled Italian revolutionary Antonio Panizzi (1797-1879), made a sketch of the sort of new reading room he wanted and

The British Museum today

When it still housed the British Library, Marx would often arrive at nine in the morning and work on till closing time, at seven at night. Marx commented that: 'The enormous amount of material relating to the history of political economy assembled in the British Museum, the fact that London is a convenient vantage point for the observation of bourgeois society … induced me to start again from the very beginning and to work carefully through the new material'. Herein lay the reason for the almost exponential growth of his project, which would result in Capital.

showed it to Robert Smirke, the designer of the Museum Building. The result was one of the world's most famous – and useful – rooms, the great domed reading room, perhaps the best-known section of the British Museum. The new library was opened in 1857, by which time Marx had already left Dean Street for the suburbs. It is recorded that on opening day a champagne breakfast was laid out for readers on their desks. By 1890 it was receiving 900,000 visitors each year.

A few years after the library opened, French writer Hippolyte Taine left this impression:

> The library contains 600,000 books: there is a huge Reading Room, circular and topped by a cupola, so arranged that no reader is far from the central bureau or has the light in his eyes. The surrounding shelves are filled with reference books, dictionaries, biographical collections, classics in every field, very well arranged and which one can consult on the spot. Moreover, on every table there is a small map or plan to show the order and position of these books. Each desk is isolated. You have nothing but the wood of your desk under your eyes and are not disturbed or bothered by the stares of a neighbour. The chairs are of leather and the desks are covered with leather too; all very neat and clean. Two pens to each desk, one quill and one steel. There is a small bookrest so that you can have a second book conveniently to hand or the book you are copying from. To get a book you write the title on a form which you hand in at the central bureau: a library clerk brings it to your own desk, and that very quickly; I tried this out and proved it, even with very rare books. You are responsible for the book until you have got the form back.

Carlyle, Thackeray, Dickens, Mazzini and Ruskin all sat in this Reading Room, and Marx, one of the most diligent readers, was to be followed by hundreds more, by Kropotkin, Shaw, Lenin, Gandhi and Govan Mbeki. Leon Trotsky was a frequent visitor to London during the early 1900s; but during his long and sad exile from the USSR his application for a reader's ticket was blocked by Churchill and the British Home Office. W.B. Yeats, who spent many of his days at the British Museum, felt that he must have been very delicate in comparison with his predecessors, for he remembered 'putting off hour after hour consulting some necessary book because I shrank from lifting the heavy volumes of the catalogue'. On one occasion, George Bernard Shaw was observed consulting at the same time *Capital* and the orchestral score of Wagner's *Tristan & Isolde*.

The only natural light in the Reading Room was from the glass dome, so when darkness came – extremely early on a foggy day (and the fogs of mid-Victorian London were notorious, as Dickens pointed out in the memorable opening pages of *Bleak House*) – reading became nearly impossible. In 1880 electric lighting was installed, but even that sometimes failed.

After obtaining his Reader's ticket in June 1850 – which was then quite an arduous task – Marx began by spending three months diligently reading back numbers of the *Economist*, followed by other periodicals and pamphlets. After years of patient research in the Reading Room, he was to end his life knowing far more about the history of political economy in Britain than most professors of the subject. Today, the Reading Room is open to all visitors to the British Museum, since the British Library is now housed in a new building. A small display of Marx's books – which can be found just to the left of the main entrance to the Reading Room – recalls his time there.

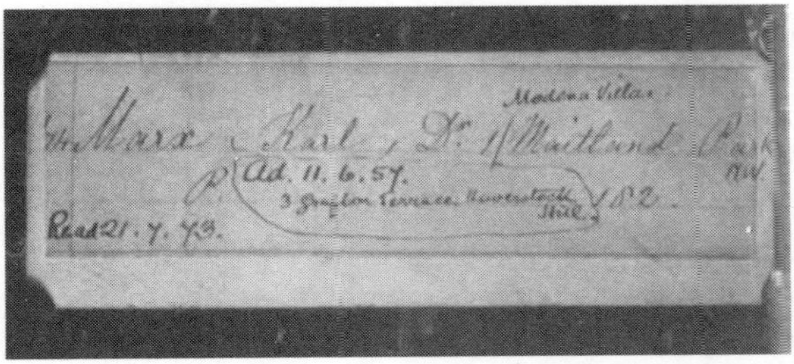

Marx's signature and address in the Reader's Book in the British Museum, 21 July 1873

Marx's seat in the Reading Room of the British Museum

Although the interior of the rotunda has been comprehensively renovated, since the 1860s, the seat numbering remains the same. This seat, number 07, is traditionally held to have been Marx's favourite.

During the mid-1860s when his health was breaking down, and he was plagued by boils, Karl spent a lot of time reading textbooks on medicine, claiming to know more than any physician about the subject. He prescribed harsh cures for himself, including creosote, opium and arsenic, taken regularly and for a long time.

It was in the old Reading Room that Karl worked on the *Address of the Central Committee to the Communist League* (1850); on *The Class Struggles in France* (1850); and the *Eighteenth Brumaire of Louis Napoleon* (1852). However, he increasingly found the demands of the *New York Daily Tribune* for the fresh articles that constituted his only paid employment to be a grinding distraction that took him away from what he considered to be his life's work. 'The continual newspaper muck annoys me', he complained. 'It takes a lot of my time, disperses my effort and in the final analysis is nothing'.

It was in the new Reading Room – where legend has it that his favourite seat was number 07 – that Marx spent the most productive period of his life, working on two fascinating projects which must have made the dispersal of effort particularly galling. The first of these was his *Grundrisse* (literally the 'outlines' of his critique of existing political economy), which was not to become known in his lifetime; while the second was, of course, his most famous project of all, *Das Kapital*, volume one of which was published in German in 1867.

The *Grundrisse*, though it ranged widely over many economic and philosophical topics, was directly influenced by the financial crisis of 1857, which interrupted the relative prosperity of mid-Victorian England and seemed to some to herald the toppling of the capitalist system. The *Grundrisse* also developed Marx's philosophy further; arguing that the patterns of thought encouraged under capitalism were as impermanent, and distorting, as the system itself. It is notable that there is a great deal in the *Grundrisse*, especially in terms of the application and benefits of new technology, that remains strikingly relevant. For Marx, automation, under the right circumstances and communal ownership, could result in greater opportunities for leisure and self-fulfilment for the many, rather than simple monetary profits for the few. The individual would thus be freed to develop to the full their potential. Such was Marx's utopia.

Das Kapital is a remarkable book, the product of Marx the system builder; anxious to understand both the structure and the dynamics of capitalism throughout its history. It is a massive book, beginning with economic theory and proceeding with history; yet the reader soon learns that the economic theory and the history are intertwined throughout, in a way that Marx himself thought of as providing 'scientific underpinning for independent working class action'. Marx drew not only on his own accumulated and critical knowledge, but also, as he wrote, on 'hitherto unused *official* sources', the reports of official commissions of enquiry that had been designed not to destroy capitalism but to strengthen it, by controlling some of its more disturbing social consequences.

Building on his earlier work, Marx argued that capitalism ultimately contained the seeds of its own destruction. He concluded the first volume with a bold assertion that:

> Along with the constantly diminishing number of the magnates of capital, who usurp and monopolise all advantages of this process of transformation, grows the mass of misery, oppression, slavery, degradation, exploitation: but with this too grows the revolt of the working class, a class always increasing in numbers, and disciplined, united, organised by the very mechanism of the process of capitalist production itself. The monopoly of capital becomes a fetter upon the mode of production, which has sprung up and flourished along with, and under it. Centralisation of the means of production and socialisation of labour at last reach a point where they become incompatible with their capitalist integument. This integument is burst asunder. The knell of capitalist private property sounds. The expropriators are expropriated.

The later volumes appeared after Marx's death (Volume II in 1885, Volume III in 1894, almost thirty years after Volume I), and were edited by Engels from the notes that Marx had left behind him. Volume IV, which appeared as *Theories of Surplus Value,* was edited by Karl Kautsky (1854-1938) after Engels had died. The first English edition of Volume I was not published for twenty years, although Marx had hoped that a

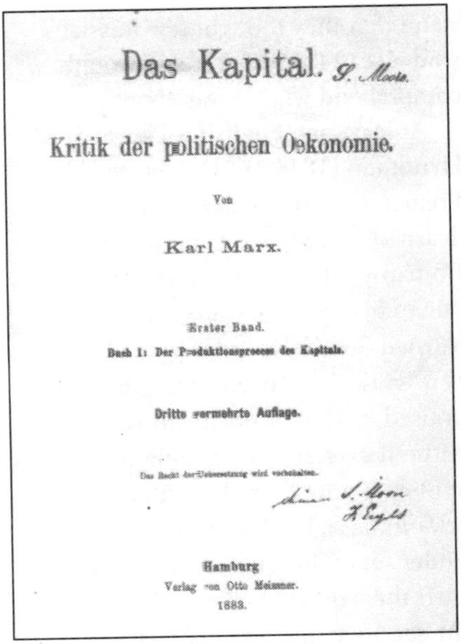

Das Kapital.

Kritik der politischen Oekonomie.

Von

Karl Marx.

Erster Band.

Buch I: Der Produktionsprocess des Kapitals.

Dritte vermehrte Auflage.

Das Recht der Uebersetzung wird vorbehalten.

Hamburg

Verlag von Otto Meissner.

1883.

The title page of the first volume of Das Kapital, 1883

This particular edition was owned by Samuel Moore, who translated the book into English, with the assistance of Engels. Both men signed the page and Engels's small, neat, hand contrasts strongly with the largely illegible, spidery writing of Marx's original manuscripts

publisher in England would guarantee sales and improve his 'miserable material condition'. The book did, however, receive a number of favourable reviews, one of which, in the *Atheneaum*, described him as 'the prophet of the working class'.

When *Das Kapital* was translated into Russian, the Russian followers of Marx were fearful lest the Tsarist censor should ban the book. Yet they need not have bothered. The censors read it and found it so hard to understand that they thought few Russians would read it and fewer still would comprehend what it was about.

At least one English socialist, H.M. Hyndman (1848-1921), who read it in French, told Marx that he had 'learned more from its perusal than from any other book I ever read'; and one of his fellow socialists actually learned French in order to read it. Few works have been so much praised, and so easily dismissed, without ever actually having been studied. Jenny Marx lamented 'that seldom has a book been written under more difficult circumstances … If the workers had an inkling of the sacrifice that was necessary to complete this work, written only for them and in their interest, they would perhaps show a bit more interest'.

It certainly has the reputation of being a difficult text, and for good reason, as Marx was actually forging the very vocabulary with which we discuss and interpret capitalist production to this day. Yet if it is difficult, it is also revolutionary, in every sense of the word, in its treatment of the relationship between the workforce and those who own the means of production – the machinery, buildings and capital. To put Marx's theory of surplus value into a typical contemporary context: after the first six hours at work, the labour of an employee who works an eight-hour day has produced goods or services that are equal in value to his or her salary, together with the costs of the process. For the remaining two hours of the day, the worker creates additional value even though he or she is not rewarded. It is this extra profit that Marx calls 'surplus value', and it goes straight to the employer, even though they have done nothing to create it. Though this process can be more difficult to discern in today's global economy, dominated by large multinational companies, where few workers come in to contact with their actual bosses, and where production is often out-sourced to different parts of world, it is no less valid or galling for going unseen.

How to get there

British Museum, Great Russell Street, WC1

By underground – Holborn Station (Central or Piccadilly Lines); Tottenham Court Road Station (Northern or Central Lines); Russell Square Station (Piccadilly Line); or Goodge Street Station (Northern Line, Charing Cross Branch)

By bus – routes 7, 8, 10, 19, 22b, 24, 25, 29, 38, 55, 68, 73, 91, 98, 134, & 188

Details of opening times can be found on the British Museum website: www.thebritishmuseum.ac.uk

British Library, 96 Euston Road, NW1

By underground – Euston Station (Northern and Victoria Lines) or Kings Cross Station (Northern Line, Bank Branch; Piccadilly, Circle, Metropolitan & Hammersmith and City Lines)

By bus – routes 10, 30, 73 & 91.

Full details can be found on the British Library Website:

7. Escape to the suburbs

While Karl worked in the British Museum, Jenny stayed behind in Dean Street. In 1856 she inherited £150 from an uncle in Scotland; and shortly afterwards, on the death of her mother, she acquired a further inheritance of £120. In those days this was quite enough to get the family out of what she called the 'evil, frightful rooms' in Dean Street and into 'a small house at the foot of romantic Hampstead Heath, not far from lovely Primrose Hill.' 'When we slept in our own beds for the first time, sat on our own chairs and even had a parlour with second-hand furniture', she wrote, 'then we really thought we were living in a magic castle'.

Number **9 Grafton Terrace,** Fitzroy Road, Kentish Town, remains much as it was when Marx first saw it. A few years later, amid the general 'tidying up' of addresses in expanding London, the name Fitzroy Road disappeared – to be found elsewhere in the district – and Grafton Terrace extended in length and changed its numbering. Number 9 became number 38, and then 46. It is a narrow three-storey 'town house' in a terrace, with a basement and a tiny back garden. The front door is reached by a steep stone staircase from the pavement. The street itself remains unusually broad, and has a grand, spacious look. In 1856 it was very new, having been built in 1849 on open fields.

46 Grafton Terrace, today

The Marx family lived at this house from October 1856 to March 1864. It was here that Marx wrote his Critique of Political Economy and the manuscript that was later edited together as The Theory of Surplus Value. Whilst living here, Karl's wife, Jenny, contracted smallpox from which she never fully recovered.

Nearby Grafton Road is one of eight in London. There are in addition a Grafton Crescent and a Grafton Yard within two miles, and, further away, Grafton Mansions, a Grafton Street, Grafton Way, Grafton Square, Grafton Gardens and Grafton Close, all elsewhere in London. The dukes of Grafton were descended from Henry Fitzroy, a natural son of King Charles II (hence the other half of Marx's address), who was given a large manor house that now lies underneath Euston Station. His promising military career was cut short when he fell at the storming of Cork, in 1691, and a large number of London street names subsequently attested to his fame, and to the influence of his descendant Augustus Henry, third Duke of Grafton, who was Prime Minister from 1766-70.

Once settled into the suburbs, Marx sometimes gave his address as Haverstock Hill, the main road linking Chalk Farm with Hampstead Village. Today, as then, Grafton Terrace is still on the 'wrong' side of that road, being very much part of the working-class district of Kentish Town, rather than the middle-class parts of Hampstead on the other side. Some working-class people had already moved out to Kentish Town by 1866: when a newspaper reporter asked a local inhabitant what had happened to people displaced by the building of a main railway line, he got a gritty and comprehensive reply: 'Some's gone down Whitechapel way, some's gone in the Dials [i.e. Seven Dials, then a notorious slum in the centre of London]; some's gone to Kentish Town, and some's gone to the Workhouse'.

There was a sense of openness about Kentish Town. When the Marxes moved there, it was described as 'throwing out lines of bricks and mortar to meet its neighbours, Hampstead Heath and Downshire Hill'. Once recommended by doctors as a salubrious place, it had been in social decline in the 1830s, but, paradoxically, it was saved by the coming of that great despoiler of the environment, the railway. The North London Railway had made little impact in the early 1850s, even when it connected Hampstead and Kentish Town with Richmond in the south-west, and Broad Street in the City. However, in the 1860s, when the Midland Railway arrived, the map of Kentish Town was altered forever, as streets were halted by great brick viaducts and the whole district was carved up into isolated sectors, leaving a sizeable tract of land with no human habitation whatsoever. Yet the slums were cleared and the rents steadily rose. Parts of the district were unmistakably middle-class.

Marx's house in Grafton Terrace, like so many of its kind, was rented. Because of the tendency of the building trade in London to overproduction, there was usually an abundance of new houses at quite low rents for middle-class tenants, and a glut of houses would bring rents well down. Thus, the Marxes paid only £36 a year in rent, in half-yearly instalments, for a house with a rateable value of £24. Of the initial rate instalment of £4.20, £3.20 was for the Poor Rate, 10p for the sewers, 20p for lighting and water, and a general rate for paving and other services. During this period the Marxes always paid their rates on time.

Even when Marx died, in 1883, only a quarter of London's houses had a constant water supply; most working-class tenants had only a single tap for the whole block; drainage was often faulty; and one water closet was usually shared by dozens of families. By contrast, the small house in Grafton Terrace had the luxury of two water closets.

For Marx, and for many others, Kentish Town was a thoroughly respectable middle-class address. For the first time since his family had been evicted from Anderson Street, eight years earlier, they were now to dwell in decent surroundings amid respectable folk. But if Marx had attained middle-class status by moving to Grafton Terrace, he had not altered the relationship to money that characterised his whole life. The long-suffering Engels, who had so often come to the rescue in Soho days, was called upon yet again: 'Today I am actually worse off than I was five years ago when I was wallowing in the very quintessence of filth', Karl wrote in 1857 – a year when England, too, was in deep financial crisis. A year later he borrowed £4 from Schapper and also tried to raise sums from moneylenders. 'The root of the trouble', he claimed plaintively in that year, 'is that my modest income can never be used to pay for what I need *next* month. The money is absorbed by regular expenses such as rent, school fees, and payment of interest to the pawnbroker'.

There were other problems too. The house in Grafton Terrace had 'the four characteristics the English like in a house', wrote Jenny. It was 'airy, sunny, dry and built on gravely soil'. Yet, in spite of the dramatic view (on a clear day the Marxes could look down to St Paul's), there was as yet no proper road leading to the house and in the wet the mud was deep. And life in the suburbs could be lonely. Jenny had few friends, and the family – like most suburban families – was isolated, and dependent on its own company. 'I often missed the long walks I had been in the habit of making in the crowded West End streets, the meetings, the clubs and our favourite public house and homely conversations', she confided to a friend.

After less than two years in Grafton Terrace, the shine had well and truly worn off: 'The situation is now completely unbearable', Marx wrote to Engels, '… I am completely disabled as far as work goes, partly because I lose most of my time in useless running around trying to make money and partly … because my power of intellectual concentration is undermined by domestic problems. My wife's nerves are quite ruined by the filth'.

On at least one occasion Karl tried to find paid employment, other than freelance newspaper work, and applied as a clerk with the Great Western Railway, only to be rejected because of his bad handwriting.

Grafton Terrace concealed more than respectable poverty. Karl also chaffed at the constraints imposed by his family, confiding in Engels that 'there is no greater absurdity than for people of general aspirations to marry and surrender themselves to the small miseries of domestic and private life'. One of the miseries was occasioned by the smallpox that ravaged Jenny in 1860; so that for a time the children were moved out to stay with the Liebknechts, also living in Kentish Town. Later, at the age of six, Eleanor had jaundice, turning the whole family, as she put it, into her 'bond slaves'. Further miseries were in store for Marx himself, who suffered tortures from crops of boils all over his body. He bore his afflictions with courage, although he naturally told Engels all about them, and about his disorders of eyes, liver and 'nerves' – which at least made a change from the constant complaint of poverty.

In 1861, Marx lost a major source of livelihood when the *New York Daily Tribune*, caught amid the outbreak of the American Civil War, cut down the number of articles it required from him. In the following year it ceased its connection with him. Again he turned to his Dutch uncle, Lion, for help, this time successfully. He also borrowed £250 from Ernest Dronke, an old friend from his days in the Communist League. Yet in January 1863 he was complaining to Engels that he intended to go bankrupt, to turn his elder daughters into governesses, to dismiss Lenchen, and to move into a lodging house with his wife and Eleanor.

Eleanor Marx as a young girl

Marx's youngest daughter was fascinated, in roughly equal parts, by theatre, the arts, and revolutionary politics. She would later assist in translating the first volume of Das Kapital in to English and became, in her own right, a very significant figure in the struggle for women's rights.

The plaque erected to Marx by Camden Council on the site of his house at 41 Maitland Park Road.

At the time this photograph was taken in 2006 a young Russian couple occupy one of the council flats in this block, having come to London in search of new opportunities following the collapse of the USSR. They were amused by, but not unsympathetic to, the historical associations of their new home. Today, just as then, London is a dynamic and constantly evolving setting for new immigrants and cultures.

Just when most necessary, new sources of income arrived. In the middle of the winter of 1863-64 he received a substantial bequest on his mother's death of almost £600, and in May 1864 his old friend in Manchester, Wilhelm Wolff, whom he had first met in Brussels in 1846, died, leaving him the residue of his estate – over £800 (Engels was left £100).

Soon the Marxes were able to move around the corner to an altogether larger, detached house, **1 Modena Villas**, to be renamed **1 Maitland Park Road**. The Maitland Park Estate had been developed between 1845 and 1855 – you can still see the remains of the old Orphanage gateway – and the Marxes were comfortable there. The Villas were demolished in 1900, and replaced by a six-storey block of flats built by a private developer. This block still exists today as 'The Grange', now part of the Maitland Park Estate.

In Maitland Park Road the Marxes had two dogs, three cats and two birds, and for the first time each child had a separate room. Within a few months, the three daughters were to hold a ball for fifty of their friends. The chief delight for Karl was his study, a splendid room overlooking Maitland Park. His future son-in-law, Cuban-born Paul Lafargue (1842-1911), visited the house for the first time in 1865 and described it in detail:

> Opposite the window and on either side of the fireplace, the walls were lined with bookcases filled with books and stacked up to the ceiling with newspapers and manuscripts. Opposite the fireplace on one side of the window were two tables piled up with papers, books and newspapers; in the middle of the room, well in the light, stood a small, plain desk (three foot by two) and a wooden armchair and the bookcase, opposite the window was a leather sofa on which Marx used to lie down for a rest from time to time. On the

> mantelpiece were more books, cigars, matches, tobacco boxes, paper-weights and photographs of Marx's daughters and wife, Wilhelm Wolff and Friedrich Engels.

Not surprisingly, such comfort and space did not come cheaply – the house was twice as expensive to run as 46 Grafton Terrace – and Karl felt 'as hard-up as a church mouse': as early as January 1866 he was grumbling that he had 'minus zero' to sustain his family. In 1868, when financial problems were looming large again, he was summoned for non-payment of rates. He justified his way of life often to Engels, once writing that he was sustained in his difficulties by the thought that 'we two are executing a combined task in which I give my time to the theoretical and party political side of the business'. 'A purely proletarian set-up would be unsuitable here', he went on, 'however fine it might have been when my wife and I were alone or when the children were young'.

When Engels retired from business in 1869 he secured Marx's position by providing him with £100 in capital to pay off his debts and an allowance of £350 a year in quarterly instalments. Thereafter, the Marxes were able to keep up appearances as they wished. Indeed, by the late 1860s, Karl was a respected figure in the neighbourhood. The St Pancras Vestry Minutes record also that in March 1868 the General Purposes

Marx's study at 1 Maitland Park Road.

This was where Marx completed the first volume of Kapital. The study was reconstructed in this model made for the Marx-Engels Museum in Moscow. The museum was closed down following the collapse of the Soviet Union in 1991, and the current whereabouts of the diorama are unknown.

The exterior of 41 Maitland Park Road, shortly before its demolition in March 1958

Committee had included him in a list of seventy ratepayers whom it wished to enrol as 'Constables for the said Parish for the ensuing year': 'Ward 1 … Charles Marx, 1 Modena Villas'. As a foreigner, Marx was quite happy to refuse. However, when six years later he applied for British citizenship, the Home Office refused him on the basis not of local evidence but of a police report that he was 'the notorious German agitator who had not been loyal to his own king and country'.

The Marxes hoped that their children would 'enter into connections which can secure them a future'. They had doubts, therefore, when Laura married Lafargue in April 1868 and moved to Paris (her mother wished that she had married an Englishman

Two shots of the derelict interior of 41 Maitland Park Road, in the spring of 1958.

Marx lived and worked in these upstairs rooms.

or a German, not a Frenchman, and in the light of her own experiences did not wish her daughters to become 'political wives'). Five years later, Eleanor, whose future was also causing them anxiety, obtained a teaching post at a boarding school in Brighton. In 1872, Jenny, the eldest daughter, married Charles Longuet (1833-1903), a survivor of the Paris Commune, a French socialist and a London medical student. Marx thoroughly approved of their union.

In 1875 the Marxes moved for the last time, just along the road to **41 Maitland Park Road**. This house was bombed in the Second World War, however, and was so badly damaged that it had to be pulled down. During the late 1950s the entire site was cleared, and is now occupied by four-storey blocks of flats erected by the former London County Council. The passage of these flats from municipal to privatised ownership in recent times is certainly something that Marx would have regarded with the deepest suspicion and regret. Since the time when the Marx family lived there, there has been as much change in the old suburbs of London as in the centre of the city, although the railway territory remains largely the same. The places that have changed least, as Liebknecht noted, are the places of recreation, and these played an important part in the life not only of the Marx family but of Karl himself.

How to get there

Grafton Terrace (Fitzroy Road), NW1; and Maitland Park Road (Modena Villas), NW3

By underground to Chalk Farm Station (Northern Line)

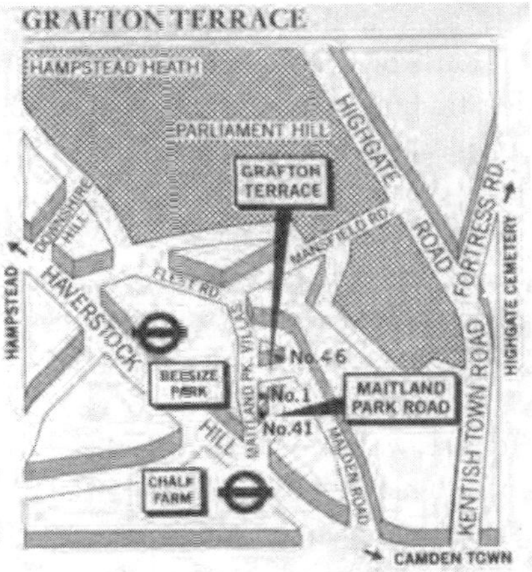

8. High days and holidays

By Bus – routes 24, 31, 168

Life for revolutionary exiles in England was not all one long slog of making and unmaking revolutions. Indeed, Liebknecht first encountered Marx not at a political meeting, but at a summer picnic of the German Workers' Education Society. Engels, exiled in smoky Manchester, liked nothing better than to follow the traditional pursuit of the English country gentleman – fox hunting – in his case with the Cheshire hunt.

Karl's own leisure pursuits were less traditional, but essentially those of a typical German academic, and in his early years in London he fenced at a 'salon' in Rathbone Place, off Oxford Street. His taste for wine, like that of Engels, also dated back to his student days. With a public house, the Lord Southampton, at the corner of Grafton Terrace, we can only surmise that many a happy hour was spent inside. Liebknecht mentions other inns, including 'the Old [Mother] Red Cap so called from a picture of little Red Riding Hood … and the Mother Shipton' (in Camden Town). He himself lived a short distance away, at 3 Roxburgh Terrace, in Kentish Town; while the 'Old Mother Red Cap' is recalled in the 'World's End' pub opposite Camden Tube Station.

Liebknecht also described a drinking spree in central London, when he, Marx and fellow German exile Edgar Bauer visited every single public house along Tottenham Court Road. Today Tottenham Court Road is mainly known as a place to buy furniture and electronic equipment, and there are comparatively few pubs, but the rate books reveal a total of eighteen in the 1850s. The three revolutionaries were soon thrown out of the last pub, after being drawn into a typical pub argument about the rival claims to fame of England and Germany. This did not lower their spirits, and after a policeman heard them smashing street lamps, they had to rely on Karl's intimate knowledge of the topography of central London to shake off the police and make their way home and not to prison.

Beer, not wine, seems to have been Karl's main drink at this time, as it was of English workingmen. Between 1830 and 1869 beer houses could be opened without a licence from the Justice of the Peace, and very heavy drinking was prevalent. Despite his own tastes, Engels described 'intemperance in the enjoyment of intoxicating liquors' as the principal failing of the English working classes.

He witnessed, at first hand, the devastating impact of alcohol upon the life of poor immigrant families in the streets of Manchester.

In one of the most popular surveys of London, in 1851, Charles Knight claimed that 'beer is to the London citizen what the water in the reservoirs of the plains of Lombardy is to the village peasantry'. Of course, the fact that London water was so unhealthy made the work of the Metropolitan Free Drinking Fountain Association as suspect to the populace as that of the brewers, with the great philanthropist Lord Shaftesbury noting as late as 1871 that there was scarcely a pint of water in London which was 'not distinctly unhealthy'.

Marx, who took part in a Hyde Park demonstration against the Sunday Observance laws, which Shaftesbury supported, loved the commodity which often went with beer: tobacco. He was a 'passionate smoker', particularly of cigars, and the various homes he inhabited must have been heavy with stale tobacco smoke. Most of the cigars he smoked were very cheap, and he liked to 'save' money by insisting on the lowest price brands. Still, he once joked that the royalties from writing *Das Kapital* would not pay for all of the cigars he had smoked while working on the volumes. It was perhaps to get away from the smoke of his own house, as much as the smoke of central London, that the Marxes, when they lived in Soho,

A picnic on Hampstead Heath, May 1864

Excursions to Hampstead Heath were a treat for the Marx family. In this Daguerrotype, Engels and Marx stand either side of the young Laura, Eleanor, and Jenny.

would escape each Sunday northwards to the green fields of **Hampstead Heath**. There, at least, he was able to relax.

'A Sunday on Hampstead Heath was the highest pleasure to us', wrote Liebknecht:

> The children spoke of it all week and grown people too anticipated it with joy. The trip itself was a feast. From Dean Street, where Marx lived, it was at least an hour and a quarter, and as a rule, a start was made as early as 11 a.m. … some time was always consumed in getting everything in

Jack Straw's Castle, Hampstead, as it was in the post-war period

This was a favourite public house of Marx and his friends.

readiness, the chicken cared for and the basket packed. That basket … it was our commissary department, and when a man has a healthy strong stomach … then the question of provisions plays a very large role. And good Lenchen knew this and had for often half-starved and, therefore, hungry guests a sympathising heart. A mighty roast veal was the centrepiece hallowed by tradition for the Sunday in Hampstead Heath.

Liebknecht's description is detailed enough to give an almost complete picture of a London Sunday, far away from the empty central streets and the closed entertainments, and what he wrote of trips to the Heath in the Dean Street days was equally true of the early days in Kentish Town.

Jack Straw's Castle, Hampstead, in January 2007

The public house closed down in 2004 and underwent a major re-development, which saw its Dickens room – recalling that writer's association with the building – stripped out. When it re-opened, the rear of the building had been converted into luxury flats.

> The march itself was generally accomplished in the following order. I led in the van with the two girls – now telling stories, now executing callisthenics … Behind us some friends. Then the main body of the army, Marx and his wife and some Sunday guest requiring special attention. And behind these Lenchen … Once arrived on the Heath, we would first choose a place where we could spread our tents at the same time having due regard to the possibility of obtaining tea and beer. But after drinking and eating their fill, as Homer has it, the male and female comrades looked for the most comfortable place of repose or seat; and when this had been found he or she – provided they did not prefer a little nap – produced the Sunday papers they had bought on the road, and now began the reading and discussing of politics – while the children, who rapidly found comrades, played hide and seek behind the heather bushes. But this easy life had to be seasoned by a little diversion, and so we ran races, sometimes we also had wrestling matches, or putting the shot (stones) or some other sport … The walk home from Hampstead Heath was always very merry, although a pleasure we have enjoyed does not, as a rule, awaken as agreeable feelings as one we are expecting. Against melancholy – although there were only too many good reasons for it – we were charmed by our irrepressible humour. The misery of exile did not exist for us – whoever began to complain was at once reminded in the most impressive manner of his social duties.

If these were rural pleasures, the Marxes also enjoyed urban pleasures, and in particular the theatre. They would often walk from Haverstock Hill to Sadler's Wells in Holborn to see Shakespeare performed, and they were deeply impressed by Henry Irving, whom they saw (and heard) as Hamlet at the Lyceum in 1874. In 1877 Marx sent a Lyceum ticket for a performance of *Richard III* to a Russian exile, Peter Lavrov (1823-1900). Lavrov had survived the crushing of the Paris Commune to join Marx in the founding of the First International, and would later become a prominent spokesman for the 'Narodnik' (People's Will) movement in Russia, which assassinated Tsar Alexander II in 1881.

While Marx gave theatre tickets as gifts, his daughter Eleanor joined the New Shakespeare Society, recited in front of the Browning Society (once picnicking down the Thames with its members), and took to the stage. She had always been a lively and entertaining person. It was characteristic of her that when she was ten, and in a popular parlour game of the period produced her 'Confession', she replied to the question 'what is your idea of happiness?' – with 'champagne'.

Marx was interested in all her

doings. He was, indeed, a good and caring father. One of his favourite games was playing 'Cavalry', pretending to be a horse, with a child – as knight or hussar – borne aloft on his shoulders. Throughout his life, he saw to it as far as he possibly could that however much he and Jenny might have to suffer through their poverty, their children would not have to suffer too. Indeed, in their aspirations for their children – private schooling at the South Hampstead Ladies College, piano lessons, dancing and lots of reading – Karl and Jenny could be seen not as revolutionary, but as bourgeois parents.

Engels never had this sense of family. His free union with the Irish factory girl Mary Burns (1822/3-1863), and later – on her death – with her sister Lizzie (1827-1878), left no place for children, although Lizzie welcomed the Marx children and showed them around Manchester. Eleanor remembered one summer day when all the female members of the household were lying on the floor the whole day, 'drinking beer, claret etc … with no stays, no boots, no petticoat and a cotton dress on'; by the time Engels returned, they were 'drunk as a jelly'.

Engels used to visit Marx regularly in London, too, before he came to live there himself, and once he had to write to Jenny apologising for leading Marx astray: he received the answer that since their 'nocturnal wanderings' Marx had been confined to bed for a week with an alleged chill.

Real illness certainly affected the leisure pattern of the Marxes, as it affected the leisure pattern of most Victorians. In 1874 Marx visited the spa at Karlsbad in Bohemia (now in the Czech Republic, and called Karlovy Vary), staying – as 'Herr Charles Marx, Privatier' – at the Germanic Hotel. 'We are very exact indeed in all our "duties" [i.e. taking the waters]', wrote Eleanor, who accompanied him, 'being fully dressed and out at the "Brunnen" [springs] by six o' clock, frequently still earlier. We take long walks, and altogether get on well here'. Marx found time away from the thermal springs to go shopping for

The House at Ventnor, Isle of Wight, where Marx spent his last winter of convalescence, 1882-83

souvenirs for his family and friends. Among his gifts was an elegant cigar case, inlaid with ivory, that he brought back for Engels.

Until 1989, a magnificent museum and large statue marked Marx's visit to the spa town, but they have since been swept away, together with memorials to Yuri Gagarin and Czech anti-fascist fighters such as Julius Fucik. Fortunately, a statue to Goethe – who visited the baths no less than thirteen times! – remains.

Health reasons also took Marx to Algiers and Monte Carlo in 1881, to Geneva in 1882 and, nearer to home, to Ventnor in the Isle of Wight. Ventnor, renowned for its air, was no more a proletarian holiday resort than Monte Carlo, although it had been graced by Herzen for a whole summer in 1854. Marx's German contemporary, Karl Baedecker, described it, in his *London and its Environs, including Excursions to Brighton, the Isle of Wight* (1879), as having a winter climate 'almost Italian in its mildness'. It was, he added, 'much frequented by persons suffering from complaints of the chest'.

Another non-proletarian resort favoured by Marx was Eastbourne, developed under the patronage of the Duke of Devonshire. It was the most respectable seaside resort on the south coast, more respectable than Brighton to the west and Hastings to the east, which he also visited, or Margate, which could be approached by river down the Thames. The river world of London was a pleasure world as well as a working world, with Richmond to the west and Southend to the east.

Another very respectable place visited by the Marxes was Harrogate,

Cavendish Place, Eastbourne

Engels stayed here, while taking the air at the fashionable resort, in 1883, 1886, 1887, and 1889.

not far from Bradford and Leeds, but very different from them. It was another spa town, not a popular resort, recommended by a doctor friend. Engels once went on holiday not to Blackpool in Lancashire, but to Great Yarmouth.

Neither Marx nor Engels followed, therefore, the work and leisure patterns of 'the masses', already plain in the year of revolutions, 1848, when in the short Whitsuntide break, a yearly festival in the life of the working classes, 116,000 trippers left Manchester for the sea. By the time of Marx's death, a visit to the seaside (for very different reasons from taking the waters) had become a fact of urban life.

'The masses', 'a human ocean', figure in Liebknecht's *Memoirs* in a non-political way, when he describes a visit with two of Marx's daughters – presumably Jenny and Laura – to the Duke of Wellington's funeral procession in 1852. 'Take good care of the children! Don't mix up with the crowd', their mother warned him as he went out. Once among the crowd, Liebknecht felt himself compelled 'to resist with all my strength, trying to protect the children so that the torrent will rush by without touching them'. There was, however, a hint of a political moral in the story, as all was: 'in vain' … 'Against the elemental forces of the masses, no human strength will avail'.

How to get there

The Rising Sun, Tottenham Court Road, W1

By underground Goodge Street Station (Northern Line, Charing Cross Branch)
By bus – routes 24 & 73

Jack Straw's Castle, North End Way, NW3

By underground: Golders Green Station (Northern Line, Edgware Branch).

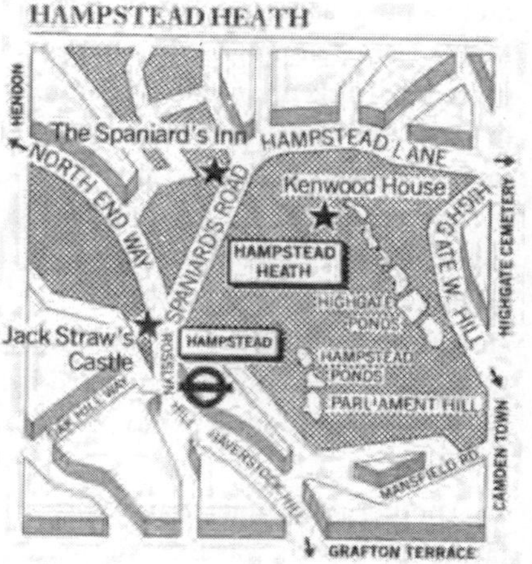

9. Revolution in Covent Garden

By bus – routes 210, 268, & 603

Covent Garden was the centre of the main political events of Marx's life during the 1860s. It is very near to London's theatre land and houses the great Opera House which was rebuilt, after a fire, in the years 1856-1888. There is no evidence that Marx ever went there, nor is there any evidence that he wandered round the famous Covent Garden fruit and vegetable market, which was moved to Battersea in 1974. The area has now been converted into a centre for tourists and shoppers. Most of the premises are occupied by fashionable boutiques, wine bars, restaurants, and advertising agencies, though there are still market stalls – selling prints, jewellery and antiques – in the market itself.

The visitors in the 1850s and early 1860s included a group of socialists, so that Covent Garden, an even more unlikely place from which to plot revolution than Soho, figures for a time as the centre of Marx's polit-

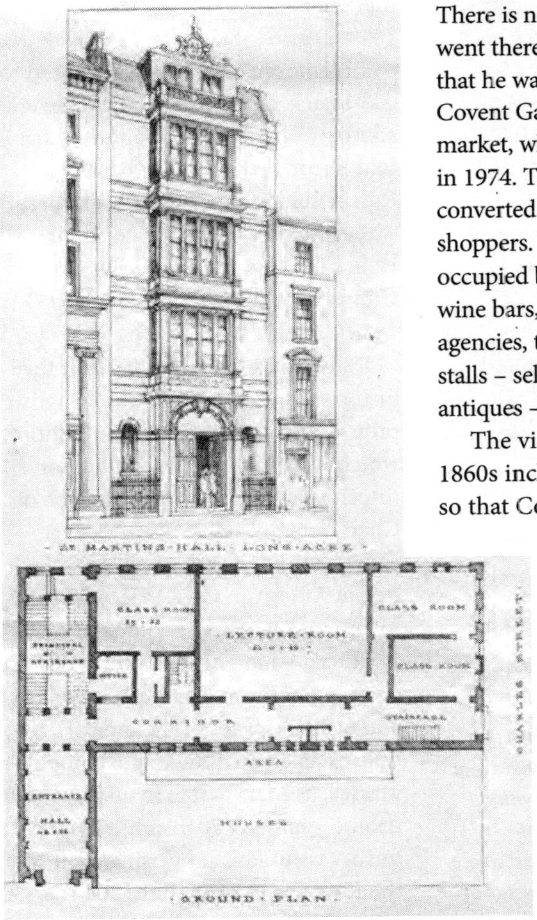

The façade and ground plan of St Martin's Hall, Long Acre

Though the building has long since been demolished, these architectural drawings show the hall as Marx and the other delegates to the First International would have known it.

ical activity. The reason why was the existence of **St Martin's Hall** in Long Acre, not far from the market, where the First International met on 25 September 1864.

St Martin's Hall, long since pulled down, had itself been rebuilt and reopened in 1862 after a fire. First opened in 1850 from the proceeds of a testimonial fund in honour of John Hullah – pioneer of 'music for the masses' – it was the scene of many concerts. It was now, not for the first time, to be used for a political appeal to the masses.

The interior of St Martin's Hall, where the International met between 1868 and 1872

Friedrich Lessner often found the sessions trying and was to recall that: 'The meetings … were as disturbing and tiring as anyone could imagine. The babble of different languages, the tremendous differences in temperament, and the variety of views – it was enormously difficult to cope with all that … those who accused Marx of intolerance should have seen at least once how he managed to grasp the thoughts of other people in flight and prove their conclusions incorrect'.

Marx had been invited to at least one of the earliest political events there in February 1855, when 'the 1848 alliance of all peoples' was commemorated, but he had refused to go because of the presence of Herzen, adding: 'I am not of the opinion that "old Europe" can be rejuvenated by Russian blood'. Two years later, there was a two-week conference at the Hall, called by the pioneering British Utopian Socialist Robert Owen (1771-1858).

1864 was a significant year in the history of nineteenth-century English protest. In particular, London politics, which had been relatively quiet for fifteen years, following the decline of Chartism, quickened again. The change in mood was partly provoked by the American Civil War, when many English workers supported the Northern Union against the slave-owning Southern Confederacy – 'new and brilliant proof of the indestructible excellence of the English popular masses', as Marx wrote in an unusual tribute – and partly inspired by the unsuccessful Polish uprising against the Russians in 1863. But 1864 was above all the year of the visit to London of the great Italian liberator

Giuseppe Garibaldi (1807-1882), who received a more enthusiastic reception from the London crowds than any visiting foreign politician had ever done. Garibaldi, who spoke at St Martin's Hall, was received by a procession of as many as fifty thousand people, who were organised by trade unionists in the London Trades Council, set up in 1860.

It is impossible to understand the ferment of the year, therefore, without taking account of the striking growth that had recently taken place in British trade unionism. The leadership of the Amalgamated Society of Engineers, founded in 1851, worked very closely with the leadership of the Amalgamated Society of Carpenters and Joiners, founded in 1860, and both of them with the Builders, who were engaged in bitter struggles with their employers between 1850 and 1861. These were the key groups in the formation in 1860 of the London Trades Council, which secured its first great success in 1861 when it persuaded the government to withdraw soldiers sent into Chelsea Barracks to replace builders on strike there.

Practical trade union concerns in the early 1860s – including the demand for a nine hour working day – suggested the need for working-class solidarity, including solidarity with workers in all parts of Britain and with workers overseas, particularly in neighbouring France – if only to check the use of cheap non-unionised foreign labour by employers. However, these practical concerns were also reinforced by political enthusiasms, for many of the protestors were interested not only in industrial legislation but, as the Chartists had been, in the right to vote.

'Never', wrote an old Chartist in 1864, 'have the relations between capital and labourers been in so disturbed and agitated a state as at the present time'. These lines appeared in the weekly *Beehive* newspaper, founded in 1861 by George Potter 'in the interest of the working classes'.

The forces of discontent converged in a great London meeting in St Martin's Hall on 25 September 1864, attended by a deputation of French trade unionists. Addresses from the working classes of one country to the other were exchanged, and it was proposed that an international association should be formed to promote peace and foster the common interests of the working classes of all countries. There had been an earlier meeting in July 1863 at St James's Hall, which had been attended by a five-man delegation from the Paris Working Men's Polish Committee, followed by discussions in the Bell Inn, the editorial headquarters of the *Beehive*. The 1864 meeting came, therefore, as a dramatic climax.

Marx had not been involved in the planning of this historic event; indeed, he had tended to avoid any direct political activity in Britain during his

Marx in Hanover, late April 1867

Marx was in Hanover from 17 April until mid-May 1867, and intended the photograph to be a birthday present to his wife. However, the local photographer – Frederick Wunder – was slow in producing the plates and, in the end, it arrived late.

long years of exile. He had concentrated on his studies and on confrontation at a distance with other European socialist theoreticians – notably P.J. Proudhon in France and his old German friend Ferdinand Lasalle, with whom he finally broke in 1860. Now, however, Marx appreciated that the workers in different countries were beginning to talk to each other as he had always demanded.

Marx sat 'mute' during the first meeting, receiving his invitation from a British trade unionist, as a representative of the German workers, only a few hours before the meeting took place. Yet it was he who drafted the Inaugural Address of what was now called the International Working Men's Association, which he described as 'a sort of review of the adventures of the working classes since 1845'.

The address was, indeed, the most important socialist document since the *Communist Manifesto*, from which it differed substantially, with most of its propositions supported by specific British evidence. It ended, however, as in 1848, with the words 'Proletarians of all countries unite'. It stated firmly also that 'the subjection of the man of labour to the man of capital lies at the bottom of all servitude, all social misery, and all political dependence'.

St Martin's Hall ultimately made way for one of the many publishers' offices that used to dot Covent Garden, among them, by coincidence, that of Odhams Press, which published the twentieth-century labour newspaper the *Daily Herald*, founded in 1911. Now most of these publishers' offices too have been demolished, and the *Daily Herald* has been defunct since 1964.

The International Working Men's Association, as constituted in September 1864, had a very eclectic membership, ranging from revolutionaries like Marx and Johann Georg Eccarius, who had worked with Marx in the Communist League; to the Positivists, the followers of the French sociologist Auguste Comte. They believed that it was important to create new forms of solidarity between workers and thinkers. One of their English leaders, Professor Beesley, took the chair at many working-class meetings, and was on good terms with working trade unionists like W.R. Cremer, the first IWMA secretary, a member of the Amalgamated Society of Carpenters and Joiners. There were twenty-seven Englishmen on its first General Council, of whom at least eleven were from the building trades.

Marx did not become a member until 5 October 1864, but five days later, when there were three French members of the Council, two Italians and two Germans, the final draft of the rules was written by Marx and completed in a late-night session at his Maitland Park house. Its provisional rules made no direct reference to Socialism, but the emancipation of the working man was identified as 'the great end to which every political movement ought to be subordinated as a means'.

The International was organised on different levels. For the ordinary trade union member his card might be his only real link. But a union, as a whole, could be centrally affiliated to the governing bodies of the International. The subjects discussed in the various sessions of the International in 1864 were wide-ranging and many of them are of more than purely historical interest. They included industrial arbitration; the past, present and future of trade unions; the fight for a shorter working day; Ireland; and European foreign policy, with one topic being defined as 'the Muscovite invasion of Europe and the re-establishment of an integral and independent Poland'.

It would have been impossible for the International to have discussed this range of topics in most European capital cities in 1864. Even in Switzerland, it has been pointed out, strikes were treated as abnormalities, and in Belgium they were seen as acts of war. There was no national trade union organisation in Napoleon III's France, though strikes were made legal in 1864, and in Germany there was virtually no collective bargaining outside the printing trade. Moreover, as Robert Applegarth, the leader of the British carpenters, proudly told the delegates, 'fortunately we have no need of creeping into holes and corners lest a policeman should see us'.

The men of the International did not engage solely in earnest discussion at their first sessions in 1864. There were other distractions, too, such as a soirée on 28 September. The programme included tea at half-past seven with music from the band of the Italian Working Men's Association, followed by addresses from foreign delegates, songs from a German chorus and, at half past ten, 'dancing – 3 polkas, 3 quadrilles and 12 other dances'. And, to help the evening along, 'wines, spirits, ales, stout, tea, coffee, etc', were to be sold 'at tavern prices'.

Between the subsequent annual assemblies of the International held in different places in Europe, it was left to the General Council in London to carry on the work. It met from eight to ten o' clock, at first every Thursday evening, and then every Tuesday evening, in time for its news to reach the weekly papers. Its first meeting place was the front room of 18 Greek Street, Soho (just around the corner from Marx's old Dean Street home), rented at £12 per year. Its members were soon faced, however, with the same sort of financial problems with which Marx was so familiar, and in October 1865 they repaired to the back room, which was £2 cheaper. However, even this arrangement did not last for long. In April 1866 there was a further move to a room in the offices of the Industrial Newspaper Company in Bouverie Street, off Fleet Street, where the new newspaper of the International, *Commonwealth*, was published.

Although throwing himself deeply into the work of the International, Marx never accepted high office. When Cremer was unable to attend meetings, however, Marx's friend and loyal supporter Eccarius would take

A brief walk from Covent Garden tube, on the corner of King Street, is the site of the former headquarters of the Communist Party of Great Britain

The building was designed by the innovative radical architect, Erno Goldfinger (1902-1987), whose name was to be purloined by Ian Fleming for his eponymous villain in the James Bond novel. His building, like his reputation, has suffered badly. With self-conscious irony, it is now occupied by a large bank.

The Central Market at Covent Garden, as it is today

the chair; and Marx himself was, from the start, the corresponding secretary for Germany, the country of his birth and the one which still interested him most. This meant that he had a new link with Liebknecht – the International's 'man on the ground' in Germany – through whom he could report the progress of the movement in his homeland to the Central Council. Later, he was also given the task of being the corresponding secretary for Russia, not a country he knew from first-hand experience.

Marx saw his main task as getting the International to think and act along 'Marxist' lines. To this end, he conducted energetic and often vituperative campaigns against rival ideologists. In 1865 the followers of Mazzini were driven out of the International, and in the same year Marx wrote *Wages, Prices and Profit* as a counterweight to the growing influence of Proudhon amongst the French Socialists. 1865 was also the year in which the International was at its peak in England – the year, too, when the Reform League was founded in London to press for manhood suffrage. Six members of the General Council of the International served on the League's Permanent Committee.

The membership of the International was never very large, and the minute books, very carefully kept in a characteristically British way, report the Association's annual income in September 1865 at: 'Only £33' (which was about one fifth of Marx's annual allowance from Engels).

There was a decline in British support after the passing of the Reform Act of 1867, which extended the suffrage to many working men, and there were few further British trade union affiliations. At this time, however, the International acquired new strength on the Continent, though only for a short period. Two events in the early 1870s were to lead to its eventual demise. The Franco-Prussian War of 1870, like the First World War forty years later, showed the strength of national rather than class feeling, and this created problems for the Association. More significantly, the Paris Commune of 1871, formed by working men after the collapse of the regular French armies and the abdication and flight of Napoleon III, plunged the International into controversy. The Commune was seen by hostile observers and governments at the time as the masterstroke of the 'secret' International Association, but in fact it proved to be, simultaneously, its zenith and its nadir.

Marx's brilliant work of instant journalism on these events, *The Civil War in France*, sold very well throughout Europe, and brought Marx once again into the revolutionary limelight. Marx saw the Commune as 'essentially a working class government', with strong internationalist credentials (Poles and Germans served on its general staff), and as the blueprint for grass-roots democracy, upon which the future governance of France, from the largest city to the smallest village, might be based. Moreover, he contrasted the order and humanity displayed by the Communards with the brutality of the rival patrician government that had established itself outside Paris at the palace of Versailles.

As a result of his support for the Commune, he soon found himself, in his own words, 'the best calumniated and menaced man in London'. This statement did not betray self-pity, however, but rather a sense of pride in his actions, for, as he added in a letter: 'That really does one good after a tedious twenty years idyll in my den'.

Unfortunately, most English trade union leaders did not share Marx's view that the Commune was 'a new point of departure of world-historic importance'. Rather, they disliked what they thought of as its excesses, and separated themselves from the work of the International, so that by September 1871, when the International met for a last time in London, at an inn just off the Tottenham Court Road, there were present only refugees from France and two Englishmen.

The work of the International was also threatened from within. Lassalle's followers had wanted trade unions to be financed by the state, thus effectively removing them from independent politics; while Bakunin's anarchists – with whom Marx increasingly locked horns – opposed any form of the state, even a revolutionary one such as the Commune, and argued for the necessity of conspiratorial strategies, assassinations and bombings, to hasten their projected revolution. By way of contrast, Marx focused his attention upon assisting the Communards and the revolution that had actually occurred.

Despite all his optimism, torn by this internecine strife the International was to struggle on for only one more year in Europe. At its Hague Conference in 1872, Engels, who had not joined the Council until 1870 (and then in the unlikely role of corresponding secretary for Spain, Portugal and Italy), proposed, and the Council accepted, that the seat of the General Council be transferred to New York. In order to preserve the integrity of the International and to prevent it from falling into Bakunin's hands, Marx effectively stifled it, and within four years it was formally dissolved in Philadelphia.

How to get there

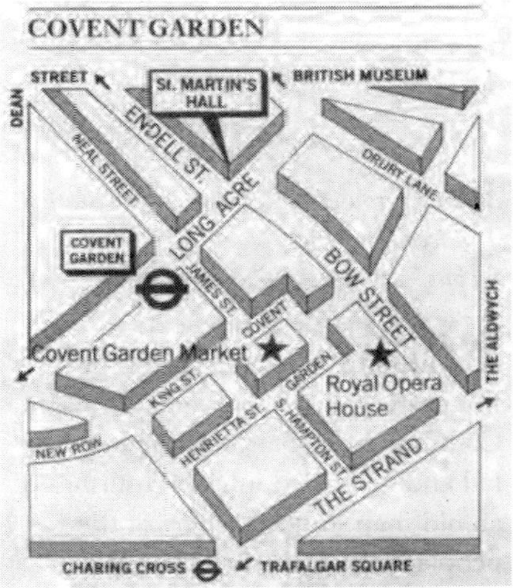

Long Acre & Covent Garden, WC2

10. Death in Highgate

By underground to Covent Garden Station (Piccadilly Line)
By bus – routes 77, 87 & 196

During the last ten years of his life, after the collapse of the International and the slaughter of the Communards, Marx's health began to fail and he settled into the routines of an old man. Indeed, many of the people he had known best had already disappeared from the scene. Some, like Joseph Moll, had been killed fighting for the revolution, but most succumbed to poverty, age, and the loneliness of exile. As early as 1864, on the death of Ferdinand Lassalle, he complained to Engels that 'the crowd is getting even smaller and no new blood is being added'. Sometimes he would attend a London funeral, like that of John Rogers, a tailor and the President of the Manhood Suffrage League, at Finchley Cemetery in 1877.

His meal times were regular and he took frequent walks on Hampstead Heath, often with his old friend Engels, who from 1870 to 1895 lived nearby at **122 Regent's Park Road**, close to Primrose Hill. Indeed, it was Jenny Marx who had helped him find the house. In the last year of his life, long after Marx was dead, Engels was to move very near to the Zoological Gardens in Regent's Park.

Like so many people of sedentary, nocturnal habits, and given to smoking and drink, Marx had misused his physique. Into his sixties he had impressed people he met as a powerful, untamed man, whose sparkling brown eyes displayed tremendous intelligence, but the last decade of his life was marked by increasingly debilitating ill health. One of the doctors he consulted attributed his complaints to poor nourishment and over-work, and prescribed regular meals, compulsory exercise and wine with soda. He also managed for a time to limit Marx's working day – when he was fit to work at all – to only two hours in the morning and two hours in the evening.

Yet Marx was restless under such conditions, and in 1875, for example, rallied himself to write a strong criticism of the Gotha Programme drafted by the German Social Democrats. Once again he attacked Lassalle's followers, but he also projected his own vision of a future society under Communism, whereby 'freedom consists in converting the state from an organ superior to society into one completely subordinate to it'. In a

The two London addresses of Friedrich Engels

Engels lived at 122 Regents Park Road (left) from September 1870 until October 1894; he then moved the short distance to 41, on the same street (below), where he lived until his death in August 1895.

passage with great resonance for the future, Marx realised that even after a successful revolution there would be enormous problems and difficulties ahead, for:

> What we have to deal with here is a communist society, not as it has *developed* on its own foundations, but, on the contrary, just as it *emerges* from capitalist society; which is thus in every respect, economically, morally and intellectually, still stamped with the birth

> marks of the old society from whose womb it emerges.

He envisaged a long process of change:

> after the enslaving subordination of the individual to the division of labour, and therewith also the antithesis between mental and physical labour, has vanished; after labour has become not only a means of life but life's prime want; after the productive forces have also increased with the all-round development of the individual, and all the springs of co-operative wealth flow more abundantly – only then can … society inscribe on its banners: From each according to his ability, to each according to his needs!

The last photograph of Marx, taken in Algiers, end of February 1882

In an attempt to restore his broken health, Marx sailed for Algiers on 20 February 1882. Taking his lead from the American, anti-Communist writer, Robert Payne: Francis Wheen sees this image as the final humiliation of a broken man. Rather, it can be seen to reflect Marx's continued good humour, self-deprecation, and fatherly concern. In dedicating the photo to his daughter, Laura, he playfully signed himself as 'Old Nick'.

Marx was also trying desperately to finish his study of *Kapital*, but his notes for the vast manuscript just swelled further, and the task was, in the end, left for Engels to complete. A Russian translation of the first volume of *Kapital* did appear in 1872, however, and Marx eagerly threw himself into a study of the Russian language, in order to better understand events in the Tsarist Empire. He also worked on translating *Kapital* into French.

The visits he made, on medical advice, to watering places and spas brought only temporary relief, for his health always broke down again as soon as he had returned to London. Moreover, to his list of troubles he had to add growing concern over his wife's worsening health. Cancer of the liver, 'a beastly illness', finally confined her to bed. 'That was a terrible time', Eleanor wrote later. 'Our dear mother lay in the big front room, Moor in the small room next to it. They who were so much to each other, whose lives had come to form part of each other, could not even be in the same room together'.

Eventually, Jenny died in Karl's presence in December 1881, her last word being an emphatic 'good'. She was sixty-seven years of age. It was a terrible blow to Marx, for, since he had been a teenager, Jenny had shared all his hopes, disappointments and hardships, as well as their many happy times together. Marx could not attend Jenny's funeral, because he had very recently been laid up in bed with pleurisy and bronchitis, and the weather was appalling. So, it fell to Engels, who had shown 'kindness and devotion that beggared description', to deliver a short speech over her grave in Highgate Cemetery.

In it he claimed eloquently that she had 'lived to see the calumny which had showered down upon her husband scattered like chaff before the wind'. Yet he offended Eleanor by saying – though she believed it, too – that Karl himself was now also dead. It was true. Karl received many warm letters of condolence paying tribute to Jenny's character and urging him to soldier on despite his dreadful loss. Yet he lived for only another fifteen months.

The final blow, from which he was never to recover, came in January 1883, with the death from cancer of the bladder of the younger Jenny, his first-born child. Again, Engels was on hand to write her obituary, and Eleanor, who travelled to Ventnor where her father was staying to tell him the news, felt that she was carrying with her her father's final death sentence.

Marx lingered on for two more months, but he now developed laryngitis and a lung tumour to add to his other complaints, and he finally died on 14 March 1883. Engels called at the house in Maitland Park Road in the afternoon and was taken by Lenchen up to the study where she had left Marx sleeping. They entered and found him dead in his favourite armchair.

Engels took care of all the funeral arrangements, sending telegrams and letters to announce the death. Marx was buried in the same grave as his

Marx's original grave in Highgate Cemetery

The plaque was later re-cut and reused as an integral part of Lawrence Bradshaw's imposing monument.

Surrounded by floral tributes, Marx's giant head stares out across Highgate

His grave remains a place of popular pilgrimage for people from across the globe. Although his physical remains are buried in London, his legacy belongs to the entire world.

wife in **Highgate Cemetery**, on 17 March 1883. About twenty people were present, among them his son-in-law Charles Longuet, who read a message in French from Peter Lavrov, in the name of the Russian Socialists. It was fitting that the funeral, small though it was, was something of an international affair.

'The greatest brain in the second half of our century had ceased to think', Engels wrote to Liebknecht, who represented the German Social Democrats at the funeral, and spoke, in German, of Marx as his 'dead, living friend'. Engels again delivered the main address at the funeral. Marx, he said, was one of the group of outstanding men, few of whom are produced in any century. 'Just as Darwin discovered the law of development of organic nature, so Marx discovered the law of development of human history'. He continued that Marx had died 'beloved, revered and mourned by millions of revolutionary fellow-workers, from the mines of Siberia to California ... His name will live on through the centuries and so also will his work'.

The grave where Karl and Jenny were laid was topped only by a simple gravestone, little more than a plaque, which recorded simply the dates of their births and deaths. Yet the cemetery itself was a place of grandeur, a typical expression of Victorian culture and wealth. It had been opened to the public two years after Queen Victoria came to the throne, in response to the over-crowded, insanitary conditions in the existing city churchyards, as a money-making concern initiated by the London Cemetery Company. Beautiful as well as profitable, it was more spacious than many residential areas, and it was also romantically landscaped, with twisting paths and sloping green banks. Its gloomy gardens with broad avenues and grandiose tombs and memorials, sculpted in many different styles and with many different symbols, demonstrate the particular attachments of Victorians (including Queen Victoria herself) to their way of death and expressions of mourning.

Marx was in good company at Highgate, where many eminent Victorians found their final resting place. The novelist George Eliot and the Chartist George Holyoake (1817-1906) are buried not far away, and there is also a memorial to Charles Dickens. And as Marx's fame grew, later generations of radicals chose to be buried close to his monument. Today, memorials to Claudia Jones (1915-1964), the founder of the Notting Hill Carnival, and Paul Foot (1937-2004), distinguished journalist and political activist, are nearby. Here also are commemorated prominent members of the Iraqi Communist Party, driven into exile by Saddam Hussein's tyranny; and a Yugoslav ambassador, who remained true to Socialism and the dream of Tito's multi-ethnic state, to the very last.

In 1954, the Marx grave was moved to a better position in the cemetery, when it was decided, though Marx had asked for a simple memorial, that a more impressive tomb should mark the spot. A tablet, now much overgrown, marks the spot of the original grave and lies approximately 100 yards to the west of the current site. Lawrence Bradshaw, an innovative post-war artist, was commissioned by the Marx Monument Committee – which was based at the Marx Memorial Library and had miners' leader Arthur Horner as its Treasurer – to design and sculpt a bronze head to sit atop the new memorial. The old gravestone was incorporated into the design, and was re-cut in order to bear the name of Eleanor, Marx's gifted daughter, whose ashes were laid to rest beside her parents. The monument was unveiled in March 1956 by Harry Pollitt (1890-1960), a life-long Marxist and the General Secretary of the Communist Party of Great Britain.

Marx's head rests on a huge Cornish granite plinth, into which is inscribed the famous exhortation from the *Communist Manifesto*, 'Workers of all lands, unite'. At the base of the monument is carved a quotation from Marx's eleventh thesis on the philosopher Ludwig Feuerbach, written in 1845: 'The philosophers have only interpreted the world in various ways. The point however is to change it'.

There have subsequently been many attempts to change the face of Marx's memorial. Slogans have been regularly daubed over it and cleaned off again, while more violent critics have tried to disfigure it, even to blow it up. It still stands, however, defiant and impervious, begging as many questions as it answers, a sight for visitors, friendly or hostile, from all

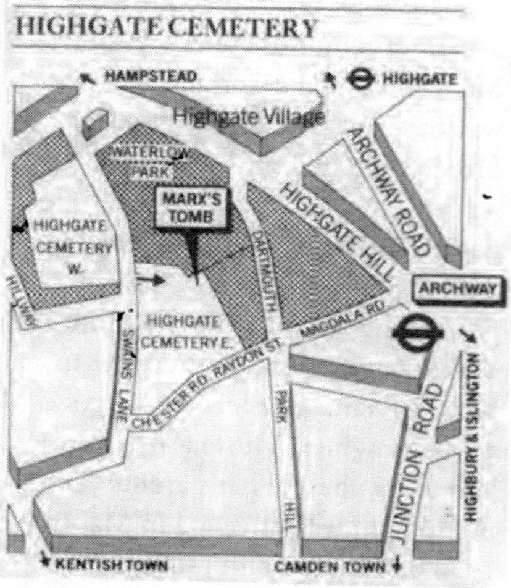

over the world.

How to get there

Marx's Tomb in Highgate Cemetery, Swain's Lane, N6

By underground Archway or Highgate Stations (Northern Line)
By bus – routes 143, 210, 214, 271 & 603.

Marx is buried in the Eastern Cemetery, which is open to visitors. The Western Cemetery, where the more imposing Victorian monuments and catacombs are located, is closed save for special tours. For information on opening times and special visits visit http://highgate-cemetery.org/.

11. After Marx

THE MARX FAMILY

Marx was survived by only two of his children. His second daughter Laura married Cuban born Frenchman Paul Lafargue, and went to live in France (Lenin later met both the Lafargues in Paris, in 1895). Sadly, the three children of the Lafargue marriage all died in infancy, and Laura died with her husband in a tragic suicide pact in 1911. Marx's youngest surviving child Eleanor had died in 1898, so that Laura was the only one of Marx's children who saw the publication of the *Theories of Surplus Value* – sometimes referred to as Volume IV of *Capital* – between 1905 and 1910.

Eleanor's interest in the theatre and her career as an actress led to her liaison with Dr. Edward Aveling (1851-1898), the socialist and scientist. She lived with him until her death in 1898, but it was an unhappy relationship. She was stunned to learn that Aveling had secretly married another woman, also an actress, under an assumed identity, and she resolved to take her own life. In this macabre episode she was assisted by Aveling, whose part in the tragedy aroused indignation in socialist circles, as many of his previous actions had done. Aveling himself died a few months later.

Laura Marx in London, 1864

Laura, like her mother before her, often acted as Marx's unofficial secretary and took notes for him.

Eleanor left no children. During her life, she had been prominent in Marxist circles in London as a member first of the Social Democratic Federation, and later of William Morris's Socialist League. She was also involved in the life of East End radical clubs in London, including the Labour

Eleanor Marx

Eleanor was a prominent organiser for the Social Democratic Federation and the joint-author of the seminal book on The Women Question. Alongside Engels, to whom she was devoted, she acted as the custodian and literary executor of her father's literary estate. Her early death, in 1898, undoubtedly robbed the working class movement of one of its most able and attractive personalities.

Patriotic Club, which had its quarters at **37c Clerkenwell Green**. She took part from there in the demonstrations on 'Bloody Sunday', 13 November 1887, and spoke at a meeting on Clerkenwell Green on 20 October 1889 in support of the London Dock Strike. She spoke at other meetings on the Green, and was active, too, in the Bloomsbury Socialist Society. In 1896 she rejoined the Social Democratic Federation and contributed regular reports thereafter to its journal *Justice*, which after her suicide published a full-page drawing of her by Walter Crane.

Both Laura and Eleanor were beneficiaries of Engels's will. Together they received three-eighths of the residue of his estate, the considerable sum of £24,000, but in a letter to them Engels asked them to hold one third of their legacy in trust for the children of their sister, Jenny Longuet, who had died ten months before Marx. There were six Longuet children, of whom

Marx and his daughter, Jenny, Margate, end of March 1866

On the advice of his doctor, Marx went to the seaside resort of Margate, on 15 March 1866, in order to recuperate. He stayed for almost a month and was joined by his eldest daughter.

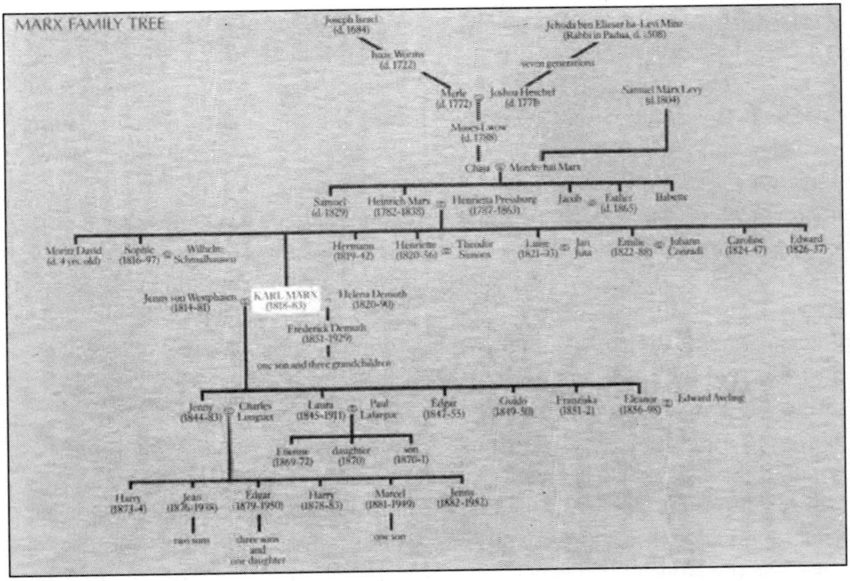

four (three boys and one girl: Jean, Edgar, Marcel, and Jenny) lived to a good age. Jean was active in the leadership of the French Socialist Party, an opponent of the First World War and a supporter, in 1921, of the so-called 'Two-and-a-half International' founded in Vienna. He, Edgar and Marcel kept the Marx family inheritance alive and were fathers to Marx's seven great-grandchildren (six boys and a girl).

Helene Demuth, 'Lenchen', the faithful family maid who had borne the trials and tribulations of the Marx family for so many years, died in 1890 and was buried in the same grave as Karl and Jenny.

Lenchen's son, Henry Frederick Demuth, received a working-class upbringing and became a skilled engineering toolmaker in East London. After the death of Marx, Helene Demuth became housekeeper to Engels, and Freddy – as he was known – was allowed to visit his mother. All three Marx sisters showed an interest in his welfare, although only Eleanor formed a close friendship with him. Freddy had a son, Harry, who provided him with three grandchildren. He died in 1929.

THE SOCIALIST MOVEMENT

Marx had died at the beginning of one of the most exciting decades of nineteenth-century English history, when the old issues of franchise politics were giving way increasingly to social politics. The country was passing through difficult economic circumstances – high unemployment, increased foreign competition, and distress in the countryside. The mid-Victorian equilibrium, always precarious, always qualified, was finally breaking down. There was talk again, therefore, for the first time since the 1840s, of possible revolution, a 'fiery furnace' through which England would have to pass. But this time much of the talk – and much of the action – focused not on the provinces, as in the 1840s, but on London, the capital. There were many radical clubs there, some of which had been founded while Marx was still alive, like the Notting Hill Progressive Club, in 1872, and the Manhood Suffrage League, which had been founded in 1875. During the 1880s there were particularly strong centres of working-class activity in Battersea, south of the river, West Ham to the north east and in dockland, where the decade ended with one of the most publicised strikes of the nineteenth century, 'the fight for the dockers' tanner' [sixpence] in 1889.

New personalities were involved in trade union and socialist struggles during the 1880s. In particular, three new political bodies turned to the propagation of Socialism: the Democratic Federation, founded in 1881 by H.M. Hyndman (1842-1921), which changed its name to the Social Democratic Federation two years later; the Socialist League, a splinter organisation created in 1885, with William Morris as one of its leaders; and the Fabian Society, which emerged from a drawing room discussion group in 1884 and which attracted personalities as different as George Bernard Shaw, H.G. Wells, and Sidney Webb.

In the trade union movement, although London was not a major stronghold, one new union of 1889 that appealed to unskilled workers – the National Union of Gas Workers and General Labourers – enrolled eight hundred men within a day of its creation, and two thousand within a week. The union had its origin in labour disturbances at the Beckton gas works in East Ham, which was then the biggest in the world. The failure of the SDF, as an avowedly Marxist party, to see the significance of this trade union growth left it curiously isolated from the main currents of political change.

Engels, who survived Marx by twelve years, watched these and other developments with great interest, although he was preoccupied with finishing *Kapital* from Marx's notes and with guiding, albeit at a distance, German Social Democracy, which in 1891 adopted a much discussed new policy document, the Erfurt Programme. Engels believed that England should have a political party as strong as the German Social Democrats were proving to be, arguing forcefully as early as 1881 – before Marx died – that 'for the full representation of labour in Parliament, as well as for the preparation of the abolition of the wages

Engels in Zurich, August 1893, at the Congress of the Second International.

In the years following Marx's death, Engels established himself as the 'Grand Old Man' of European Social Democracy. His influence was enormous, and a new generation of Socialists gathered, quite literally, around his table. From left to right: Ferdinand and Frieda Simon (the son-in-law and the daughter of August Bebel); Clara Zetkin; Engels; Julia Bebel (wife of August); August Bebel; the Bernsteins' son; Regina Bernstein; and her husband Eduard Bernstein.

system, organisations will become necessary, not of separate trades, but of the working class as a body. And the sooner this is done the better. There is no body in the world which could for a day resist the British working class organised as one'.

However, Engels had great reservations about the Social Democratic Federation, as led by Hyndman, 'the socialist in the top hat'. This was despite the fact that Hyndman took up many of Marx's ideas. William Morris's socialism had much in common with that of Marx, but he too did not impress Engels as a leader. Above all, Engels was anxious to restrain over-confident hopes of imminent revolution in the revolutionary exile circles based in London, as well as among the British labour movement. Rather, he was prepared to press flexibly for short-term objectives that would attract the voters.

Thus, socialism, while increasing in its appeal during the 1880s, was characterised by fierce in-fighting. Rank-and-file members might belong to organisations whose leaders, while agreed upon core principles, were arguing bitterly with one another. Hyndman, for example, refused to speak at a meeting arranged at Marx's grave in 1884, rather than share a platform with his opponents.

In 1893 yet another new labour party was to be founded – the Independent Labour Party – not in London but in Bradford, by the Scottish former miner James Keir Hardie (1856-1915). In 1892 he had been elected MP for West Ham, as the first London Independent Labour MP, and, although he was defeated in 1895, the new ILP was to prove far more successful as a party than the SDF. Pragmatic, rather than theoretical – and famously the product of both Marx and Methodism – it was to take the lead, along with trade unionists and other sections of the labour movement, in summoning, on 27 February 1900, a historically significant meeting at the Memorial Hall, Farringdon Street, where the Labour Representative Committee, later to be known as the Labour Party, was formed.

The years between 1883 and 1900 can be examined in detail; largely through the pages of newly founded Labour journals such as *Justice*, set up by Hyndman in 1884, and *Commonwealth*, the organ of the Socialist League, launched by Morris in 1885. The Fabians produced their volume of *Essays*, which subsequently became famous, in 1889. There was also an increasingly probing non-socialist literature about London, which acquired a new County Council in 1888. Hyndman himself assembled a mass of facts about the city and its problems, but so, too, did the non-socialist Charles Booth (1840-1916), whose massive survey, *The Life and Labour of the People of London*, which appeared between 1891 and 1903, reveals both the intense variety of human circumstances in London and the distinctive features of each of its constituent parts.

Within London, which Booth described as an 'unrivalled national emporium and mother city of the Kingdom and of the Empire', there was still a place for revolutionary exiles from across Europe. Prince Peter Kropotkin (1842-1921), the Russian anarchist, who arrived for the first time in 1876 and settled in London permanently in 1886, was one of the foremost. He was to stay in London almost as long as Marx had: returning to Petrograd only in 1917, on the wind of the February Revolution. In 1883, the year of Marx's death, another Russian exile, Sergius Stepniak (1852-1895), had arrived, and five years later Eduard Bernstein (1850-1932), who was to become a leader of German 'revisionist' Marxism. Bernstein spent more than a decade in London, leaving only reluctantly in order to take up a seat in the German Parliament.

12. The Marx legacy

Judgements that Marx's work was outdated, or disproved by the surprising durability of capitalism, are nothing new. Bernstein thought that capitalism might gradually evolve to the benefit of the working people; while Tomas Masaryk (1850-1937), the Czech nationalist leader, and later first president of Czechoslovakia, pronounced that Marxism had entered its terminal crisis as early as 1898. When, in 1920, H.G. Wells came face to face with the twin busts of Marx and Engels outside the Smolny Institute, he was thoroughly affronted by their bushy Victorian beards: they spoke to him not of progress, but of the stifled morality of the previous generation. The future, he predicted, was definitely going to be clean-shaven!

Such views are hardly surprising in view of the fact that Marx had died without seeing any signs of the revolution that he had predicted. Indeed, in the thirty years that followed his death it was the relatively respectable, parliamentary road pioneered by the German Social Democrats that seemed to be yielding the greatest dividends. All of this was to change, however, with two earth shattering events. The first was the outbreak of the Great War, in which the majority of Europe's parliamentary social democrats appeared willing to vote for war subsidies used to send their working classes to battle one another. The second was the victory of the Russian Revolution of October 1917, which seemed to offer a blueprint for the success of future revolutions and took its inspiration directly from Marx's work.

Lenin (1870-1924), the architect of the Bolshevik Revolution, was, as a young man, an exile in London. Driven from Germany and tailed by the Tsarist secret police, he came to England – at the invitation of the British Social Democrat Harry Quelch (1858-1913) – in order to maintain the publication of the revolutionary newspaper *Iskra* (the 'Spark'). 'We arrived in London in April 1902', wrote his wife, Nadezhda Krupskaya, and the 'immensity of London staggered us … Although the weather was filthy the day we arrived, Vladimir Ilyich brightened up and at once began to look round this citadel of capitalism with curiosity'. He liked going on long bus rides across town on the open top-deck of an omnibus, enjoying 'the movement of the huge commercial city' but observing its inequalities between rich and poor. Passing Big Ben and the Houses of

Parliament, he waved across the Thames to the sprawling slum tenements and sighed to his guest on the outing, 'two nations, two nations'.

Lenin and Krupskaya initially rented two small rooms in a house bordering Regent's Square. The exact address is not recorded and, with the rent running at far more than they could afford, the couple soon moved to two other, unfurnished, rooms at 30 Holford Square, which was then in the London Borough of Finsbury but is now in Islington. They stayed there until May 1903, known as 'Mr & Mrs Richter', living modestly and arousing little in the way of comment; save from their landlady, Mrs Yeo, who objected to Krupskaya not wearing a wedding ring.

Sadly, the house was flattened during a Nazi bombing raid in early 1942. As an act of solidarity and defiance, the Borough of Finsbury commissioned the gifted modernist architect Berthold Lubetkin (1901-1990), to design a monument to recall Lenin's stay. He encased a bust of Lenin, donated to the British people by the Soviet government, in a black marble surround. The monument was unveiled in front of British and Soviet dignitaries on 22 April 1942, but fell victim to the Cold War. As the site was cleared away after the war, in order to make room for new tower blocks, the bust was taken into 'temporary storage' by the Council. To register his disgust, Lubetkin had his beautiful casement sunk into the foundations of the Ernest Bevin tower block. The bust, however, does survive and can be seen in the collection of the Islington Museum. An early copy can be seen in the reading room of the Marx Memorial Library.

During his time in London, Lenin produced sixteen issues of *Iskra* – numbers 22 to 38 – which firmly established him as an influential figure within revolutionary circles. His surroundings, however, were anything but glamorous. Quelch, the editor of the British Social Democrat journal *Justice*, allowed him the use of his machines in the Twentieth Century Press, in Clerkenwell Green (now the **Marx Memorial Library**, see p 103 for more information on the library building). 'As a consequence', Lenin later wrote, 'Quelch himself had to "squeeze up": a corner had been boarded off at the print shop by a thin partition to serve him as an editorial room. This corner contained a quite small writing table, a bookshelf above it, and a chair'. There was no room for a second seat, but the two men forged a close working relationship. The *Iskra* was produced in extremely large quantities, as so many copies were seized by the secret police as it was smuggled back into Tsarist empire. The typesetting for it was done covertly at a little Russian printer's shop in the East End.

In many ways it was fitting that the *Iskra* was produced at the Twentieth Century Press, for the earliest English editions of Marx's *Wage Labour and*

Lenin's office in the Marx Memorial Library

Despite its small size, this room was the centre of production for both the Russian Revolutionary newspaper, Iskra, and for Justice, the journal of the British Social Democrats.

Capital, *The Civil War in France*, and the *Poverty of Philosophy* – which Harry Quelch, himself, had translated – had rolled off the presses there.

In the spring of 1903, the publication of *Iskra* was moved to Geneva, but Lenin returned to London in order to attend the Second Congress of the Russian Social Democratic Labour Party (held in July 1903), the Third Congress (held in April 1905), and the Fifth Congress (held in April 1907). He visited England one last time, in May 1908, when he researched at the British Library.

It was at the Second Congress that the party split into two wings: the Bolsheviks (the majority) led by Lenin, who believed that revolution could be most effectively achieved by a dedicated band of professional revolutionaries; and the Mensheviks (the minority) led by Plekhanov, 'the father of Russian Marxism', and Trotsky, who conceived of a far wider, and more open, membership. So successful were the delegates at evading police surveillance that we do not know where the Congress was actually held, though it is thought that its opening sessions were held somewhere along Charlotte Street, off Tottenham Court Road.

The location of the Third Congress, attended only by Bolshevik delegates, is similarly unknown. However, a

The Marx Memorial Library today

The library was founded as a protest against the Nazi book burnings in 1933, and as a tribute marking the fiftieth anniversary of Marx's death. From 1902-3 Lenin worked in a small office on the first floor.

London County Council plaque, erected in June 1962, marks the site of Lenin's lodgings at 16 Percy Circus, where he stayed for the duration of the Congress from April to May 1905.

The Fifth Congress, which included both Bolshevik and Menshevik delegates, was held at the Brotherhood Church, at the junction of Southgate and Balmes Roads in Islington. A Mr Swann, who had been a Church of England clergyman before resigning his benefice and becoming chief cashier of the *Daily Herald*, chaired Sunday meetings there, which mixed Bible readings with political discussion. The building is another one that no longer exists. Pacifists held meetings there throughout the 1914-1918 war and, as a result, it became a target for vandals. By 1930 it had fallen into such a bad state of repair that it was considered derelict, and its trustees could not raise the necessary funds to prevent its destruction.

English Social Democrats, ordinary Londoners, and the Jewish community based in Whitechapel, many of whose members had fled from the Tsar's pogroms in Eastern Europe, were on hand to give assistance to the delegates. George Lansbury (1859-1940), the future inter-war leader of the Labour Party, and pioneering Marxist historian

Henry Brailsford (1873-1958) helped to arrange the Congress, and secured a loan from a wealthy American industrialist, Joseph Fells, in order to finance proceedings. (Though suffering the ill effects of the Civil War, Lenin's young Soviet government was to honour this debt, in full, in 1922.)

Despite the availability of funds, many delegates were forced into cramped and extremely damp lodgings. The great Russian playwright and revolutionary Maxim Gorky and his partner Maria Andreyeva attempted to dry out sodden clothes on the radiators in their rooms in Bloomsbury; while at night, Gorky and Lenin were observed eating fish and chips, from newspapers, outside Kings Cross Station.

If the creation of a workers' state in 1917, and its maintenance for just over seventy years, propelled Marx and his theories to worldwide prominence, the collapse of the Soviet Union in 1991, with little more than a gasp, appeared to finally consign them to the dustbin of history. Across Eastern Europe and Africa monuments to Marx, Engels, and Lenin, toppled into the dust or were melted down for scrap. (In this regard, London has gone against the trend. In the decade after the collapse of the Warsaw Pact, the small number of public monuments to Marx in London actually experienced a slight, yet still notable, growth.)

In judging the past, all that Marx wrote and did remains highly relevant. In looking to the future, long-term perspectives are necessary. Capitalism has proved adaptable, but it still remains vulnerable. Communist China survived the collapse of the Soviet Union in 1991. So too Marx's influence on Cuba, Vietnam, Latin America and parts of Asia and Africa.

The bust of Nelson Mandela on the South Bank

Commissioned by Ken Livingstone and the GLC, and unveiled in 1985, this work spoke for many ordinary Londoners who wished to register their opposition to the apartheid regime. At that time, Mandela had already spent twenty-one years in a South African jail. As both a young activist and a mature statesman, he was deeply influenced by Marx's thoughts. In 2007, he would return to London to see another monument raised in his honour: this time a statue in parliament square, where he took his place alongside former British prime ministers.

Marx restored

Repairs were finished to the Soho Clock in the spring of 2007. The gaping hole in the centre of the mural was filled in, and Marx once more took his place among those Londoners whose achievements had changed not only the history of the city, but had also refashioned the world.

The commemorative plaque to Henry Hyndman at Golder's Green Cemetery

Hyndman's influence on the development of British Marxism cannot be underestimated. However, in stark contrast to Keir Hardie and many other leaders of the Labour Party, he supported the war of 1914-18, which broke apart the Second International.

In Russia and its neighbours there has been continuity as well as reaction. The perspectives of the twenty-first century are quite different from 1991. But the immediacy of protest must always be taken into account.

After his death Marx's influence extended not only into politics but into almost every contemporary sphere of human life: from great music, literature and art, to the study of economics, philosophy and history. Canvases by Picasso, plays and poems by Brecht, symphonies by Shostakovich are works which – whether directly or indirectly – bear the unmistakable imprint of Marx's ideas.

Without Marx it is practically impossible to conceive of, let alone to explain, the forces that first created, and then sustained, the Industrial Revolution. Moreover, without the knowledge of Marx's writings it is just as difficult to understand the motivations of those revolutionaries who stormed the Winter Palace in 1917, or who in 1959 swept down from the mountains to take power in Havana; and Marx makes it easier for us to empathise with the landless peasants of Bolivia and Venezuela today, who struggle to escape from poverty, injustice and the ravages of disease and hunger.

For them – and for many others around the world – the vitality and immediacy of Marx's work, which cuts across so many disciplines and defies any easy classification, continues to offer a powerful critique of the destructiveness and inherent instability of capitalism, which when unchecked manifestly stunts individual potential and thoroughly corrupts and disfigures the development of the human spirit.

A Pageant of Working Class History

Dan Jones' vision of radical Clerkenwell painted in 1985. The artist manages to convey the energy of the mass protests – from the revolutionary movements of the 1790s right down to the anti-Apartheid struggles of the 1980s – to have converged on this part of the City of London. Marx, he suggests, embodies all these facets of political thought and struggle.

In this light, rather than having failed, Marx has almost passed into common sense. So many of the core beliefs that he championed – his opposition to poverty, exploitation and oppression, both at home and abroad – which seemed strange or impractical during an age of European empires, are now mainstream ideas.

It is no longer difficult to envisage a world where the essential needs of food, clean water and shelter, together with the provision of healthcare, education and complete security – during times of misfortune or old age – could be freely available to all, without exception.

It was Marx's genius to realise that the key to this fundamental transformation lay in co-operation rather than in dog-eat-dog competition, and to devote his life to the systematic study of the corrosive economic forces that were creating a growing gap between poverty and wealth, at a time when the achievements of science and technology could have removed starvation and misery from the planet. This bold challenge remains just as important for us today as it was for Marx in 1848, when he wrote the *Communist Manifesto*.

Though his vision of equality and economic democracy still remains to be fulfilled, he was able during his lifetime to forge a new, optimistic and highly creative philosophy, that stressed the ability of men and women to make their own history, and by their own efforts to transform their dreams of a fairer and more equal society into a solid and positive reality.

Though Marx trod the streets of London, and knew its rhythms and people, his legacy belongs to the entire world. His message is universal and if, through retracing his steps, the reader of this guide comes closer to an understanding of him, the point today – as it was in Marx's day – is not just to interpret existing society, but to change it.

How to get there

Marx Memorial Library, 37a Clerkenwell Green, EC1

By underground to Farringdon Station (Circle, Hammersmith, and Metropolitan Lines)

By bus – routes 55, 63, 243 & 249

Percy Circus, WC1

By underground to Kings Cross Station (Northern Line, Bank Branch, Piccadilly, Victoria, Circler, Hammersmith, & District Lines)

By bus – routes 17, 45, 46, 63, 219 & 319

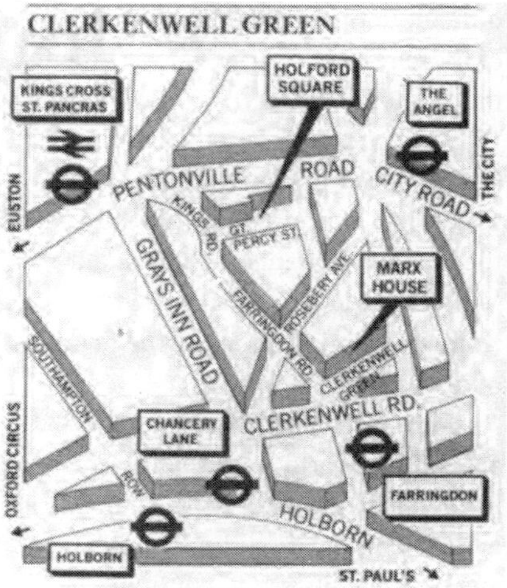

The Marx Memorial Library

The Marx Memorial Library is located at 37/38 Clerkenwell Green, in a building now known as Marx House. The building was constructed in 1737 as the Welsh Charity School, and in 1967 it was granted a Preservation Order by the Minister of Housing and Local Government, 'on historical grounds, namely its part in the Charity Schools Movement, and its association with the origins of the Radical and Socialist Movements in this country'. The building, 'neglected and almost ruinous', had been acquired in 1933 and converted into a 'Marx Memorial Library' and 'Workers' School'. The Preservation Order was conditional on the Library demolishing what was by then a commercial looking frontage and restoring the old façade: the original architect had been John Steed. After a public appeal, this was done, and as a charity the Library has subsequently received a number of valuable benefactions.

The aim of the library is the advancement of education, knowledge and learning and it holds books, peri-

The reading room of the Marx Memorial Library

odicals and manuscripts relating to all aspects of Marxism, the history of socialism and the working-class movement. It is an independent organisation, a registered charity, financed by its members and affiliates. It has some 40,000 volumes in the lending section covering a range of subjects including Marx, Engels, Lenin, the Spanish Civil War and the History of Socialism and the British Labour Movement. For more information on the library go to www.marx-memorial-library.org.

Further reading

The literature both for, and against, Marx is enormous and continually expanding. Rather than wade through the various competing, and often now quite dated theses, the best place to start is with what Marx, himself, actually wrote.

The most comprehensive and satisfying single-volume collection can be found in D. McLellan (ed.), *Karl Marx: Selected Writings*, 2nd Edition (Oxford University Press, Oxford, 2006). This contains extracts from Marx's journalism, philosophical works and economics. It also contains the full text of the Communist Manifesto.

For those wanting to study Marx in greater depth, there is the *Collected Works of Marx and Engels*, in a monumental 50 volumes (Lawrence and Wishart, London, 1975-2004). This represents the definitive English language edition, containing all of their works and known correspondence, together with full annotations. It is unlikely that it will ever be fully superseded.

The finest scholarly biography of Marx is provided by D. McLellan, *Karl Marx: A Biography*, 2nd Edition (Palgrave, Houndmills, Basingstoke, 2006). A more populist and anecdotal account is to be found in F. Wheen, *Karl Marx* (Fourth Estate, London, 1999).

Engels was poorly served by biographers until the appearance of Terrell Carver's *Friedrich Engels. His Life and Thought* (Macmillan, Houndmills, Basingstoke, 1989), which does much to free the man from Marx's long shadow and to encourage the study of his theoretical work in its own right.

For critical introductions to Marx, Jonathan Wolf's *Why Read Marx Today?* (Oxford University Press, Oxford, 2002), provides a concise and thoughtful account, which is particularly strong on his youthful writings and philosophical studies. An excellent, thought-provoking, collection of themed essays on Marx is to be found in T. Carver, *The Postmodern Marx* (Manchester University Press, Manchester, 1998).

The life of Eleanor Marx is recorded in two solid biographies by Yvonne Kapp, *Eleanor Marx, Family Life, 1855-1883* (Lawrence and Wishart, London, 1972); and *Eleanor Marx, The Crowded Years, 1884-1898* (Lawrence and Wishart, London, 1976). A collection of academic essays that examine Eleanor as feminist, socialist and literary critic is provided by J. Stokes (ed.), *Eleanor Marx, 1855-1898, Life – Work – Contacts* (Ashgate, Burlington, USA, 2000).

However unsympathetic he may be, Edward Aveling is in need of a fresh study, not least in order to disentangle the strands of his thought from his relationships with Marx, Engels and Eleanor.

A well-chosen set of family letters are collected together in O. Meier (ed.), *The Daughters of Karl Marx. Family Correspondence, 1866-1898* (Andre Deutsch Limited, London 1982).

For Victorian urban life and the development of London as a metropolis, there is A. Briggs, *Victorian Cities* (Penguin Books, Harmondsworth, 1968, rpt. University of California Press, Berkeley, California, 1993); while for an understanding of the culture and politics of Marx's day: E. Hobsbawm, *The Age of Capital, 1848-1875*, (Weidenfeld and Nicolson, London, 1975, rpt. 1996), is essential. Rosemary Ashton's *Little Germany: Exile and Asylum in Victorian England* (Oxford University Press, Oxford, 1986) discusses Marx's stay in London and sets him in context with the hundreds of other refugees who fled to England, with their families, after the failure of the revolutionary tide of 1848-49.

The seminal political biography of William Morris is found in E.P. Thompson's *William Morris, Romantic to Revolutionary* (Pantheon Books, New York, 1976); while an account of the rise of British Marxism is provided by: S. Macintyre, *A Proletarian Science* (Lawrence and Wishart, London, 1986).

A lively and accessible introduction to the life and work of Lenin is provided by Christopher Hill's account of *Lenin and the Russian Revolution* (Penguin Books, Harmondsworth, 1971). A more detailed study, by one who knew him, is to be found in: L. Fischer, *The Life of Lenin* (Weidenfeld and Nicolson, London, 1965).

For Lenin's exile in Britain and the printing of the *Iskra*, there is Andrew Rothstein's pamphlet, *Lenin in Britain* (CPGB, London, 1970). Copies of this are still available from the Marx Memorial Library, London. See: for details.

Index